PARANORMAL ROMANCE TROPES

A GUIDE FOR
BOOKSTAGRAM & BOOKTOK

PARANORMAL ROMANCE TROPES: A GUIDE FOR BOOKSTAGRAM AND BOOKTOK

E.B. BORBÓN

PARANORMAL ROMANCE TROPES

A GUIDE FOR
BOOKSTAGRAM & BOOKTOK

asturian
HOUSE PRESS

CONTENTS

1
INTRODUCTION
BOOKSTAGRAMMERS AND BOOKTOKERS

In today's digital age, social media has revolutionized the way we consume and engage with content. In the realm of books and literature, Bookstagrammers and Booktokers have emerged as influential figures, shaping trends, and creating a vibrant community of readers and book enthusiasts. In this chapter, we will explore the importance of Bookstagrammers and Booktokers, their positive impact on the publishing industry, and express our gratitude for the time and work they put into their craft.

THE RISE OF BOOKSTAGRAMMERS AND BOOKTOKERS

Bookstagrammers and Booktokers are individuals who have harnessed the power of social media platforms such as Instagram and TikTok to share their love for books. Through carefully curated photos, creative captions, and engaging videos, they have built dedicated followings of book lovers who turn to them for recommendations, reviews, and discussions.

The bookstagram community, with its visually appealing book photos, has created a space where readers can connect, discover new titles, and share their reading experiences. Booktokers, on the other hand, have embraced the short-form video format, offering quick book recommendations, reading vlogs, and lively discussions that captivate and entertain viewers.

THE IMPORTANCE OF BOOKSTAGRAMMERS AND BOOKTOKERS

Bookstagrammers and Booktokers play a vital role in the book industry by promoting books, authors, and publishers. Their influence extends beyond their immediate followers, as their content can go viral and reach a wide audience. By sharing their enthusiasm for books, they inspire others to read, reignite interest in classics, and introduce diverse voices and perspectives.

These content creators also bridge the gap between readers and authors, fostering direct connections and fostering meaningful conversations. Their reviews, recommendations, and discussions provide valuable insights and help readers make informed choices about their reading material. In a world saturated with options, Bookstagrammers and Booktokers serve as trusted curators, guiding readers towards their next literary adventure.

THE POSITIVE IMPACT ON THE PUBLISHING INDUSTRY

Bookstagrammers and Booktokers have become influential voices in the publishing industry. Their ability to generate buzz around specific titles has led to increased book sales and exposure for both established and debut authors. Publishers now recognize the value of partnering with these content creators to promote their books, often providing advanced copies and exclusive content to share with their followers.

Furthermore, Bookstagrammers and Booktokers have paved the way for marginalized voices and underrepresented authors to gain recognition. They actively seek out diverse reads, shedding light on stories and perspectives that may have otherwise gone unnoticed. This inclusivity and emphasis on representation contribute to a more vibrant and inclusive literary landscape.

EXPRESSING GRATITUDE

As writers, publishers, and readers, it is important to express our gratitude for the time and effort that Bookstagrammers and Booktokers put into their craft. Creating captivating content, maintaining an engaging online presence, and fostering a supportive community requires dedication and passion. Their contributions to the literary world should be acknowledged and celebrated.

To Bookstagrammers and Booktokers, we appreciate the countless hours spent reading, photographing, filming, editing, and engaging with the book-loving community. Your commitment to promoting literature, supporting authors, and fostering a love of reading is truly commendable. You have enriched the reading experience for countless individuals and contributed to the growth and diversity of the publishing industry.

In conclusion, Bookstagrammers and Booktokers have become integral to the book-loving community, offering a fresh and dynamic approach to sharing and discussing literature. Their influence on readers' choices, the visibility they bring to authors and diverse voices, and their overall impact on the publishing industry cannot be overstated. Let us celebrate and support these digital book ambassadors, recognizing their valuable contributions and embracing the collaborative and evolving nature of the literary world in the digital age.

2
THE APPEAL OF PARANORMAL ROMANCE

Paranormal romance is a captivating genre that blends elements of the supernatural and romance, weaving tales of love that transcend the boundaries of our everyday world. At the heart of this genre lies a rich tapestry of tropes, which are recurring themes, motifs, and storylines that have become familiar to both writers and readers alike. In this chapter, we will explore what paranormal romance tropes are, why they are important, and how they have evolved over time within literature.

WHAT ARE PARANORMAL ROMANCE TROPES?

Paranormal romance tropes are recurring themes and narrative devices that define the genre. They provide a framework for storytelling, allowing writers to delve into the realm of the supernatural while simultaneously exploring the complexities of love and relationships. These tropes often involve fantastical or supernatural elements, such as vampires, werewolves, witches, ghosts, angels, demons, and other mystical creatures.

These tropes serve as the building blocks of paranormal romance narratives, offering familiar storylines and archetypal characters that readers can connect with. From star-crossed lovers and forbidden romances to soulmates and fated encounters, these tropes provide a sense of familiarity and anticipation, drawing readers into a world where love transcends the ordinary.

WHY ARE PARANORMAL ROMANCE TROPES IMPORTANT?

Paranormal romance tropes play a crucial role in the genre's popularity and appeal. They provide readers with a sense of escapism, allowing them to immerse themselves in a world where the extraordinary becomes possible. By blending the supernatural with the emotional intensity of romance, these tropes create a unique and enticing reading experience.

Tropes also offer a sense of comfort and predictability. While each story may have its unique twists and turns, the presence of familiar tropes allows readers to have certain expectations and anticipations. They seek out paranormal romance novels precisely because they crave the emotional rollercoaster, the thrilling adventures, and the magical elements that these tropes bring to the forefront.

Moreover, paranormal romance tropes provide a means of exploring universal themes and desires. Love, desire, passion, and the search for connection are timeless human experiences. By placing these experiences in supernatural settings, paranormal romance tropes allow writers and readers to examine these themes from fresh and unique perspectives.

THE EVOLUTION OF PARANORMAL ROMANCE TROPES IN LITERATURE

Paranormal romance has a rich history that spans several decades. The genre's roots can be traced back to Gothic literature, with novels like Bram Stoker's "Dracula" and Mary Shelley's "Frankenstein" incorporating elements of romance and the supernatural. These early works laid the foundation for the fusion of romance and the paranormal, inspiring future generations of writers.

As literature evolved, so did paranormal romance tropes. In the 20th century, authors like Anne Rice revitalized the vampire trope with her iconic "The Vampire Chronicles," introducing complex, charismatic vampires that captivated readers. The werewolf trope also gained prominence with novels like Patricia Briggs' "Moon Called" and Stephenie Meyer's "Twilight" series, which showcased the allure of supernatural creatures torn between their primal instincts and their capacity for love.

The turn of the 21st century witnessed a surge in the popularity of paranormal romance, with authors like J.R. Ward, Sherrilyn Kenyon, and Charlaine Harris pushing the boundaries of the genre. Their works introduced new tropes, such as the concept of soulmates and the integration of mythological creatures, broadening the scope of paranormal romance and captivating readers with fresh narratives.

The rise of urban fantasy, a subgenre closely related to paranormal romance, also influenced the evolution of tropes. Authors like Laurell K. Hamilton and

Patricia Briggs blended elements of romance, fantasy, and mystery, creating complex worlds where supernatural beings coexist with humans, often intertwining romantic and supernatural storylines.

In recent years, paranormal romance has continued to evolve, embracing diverse characters, exploring non-traditional relationships, and incorporating themes of empowerment and agency. The genre has become more inclusive, representing a wider range of identities and love stories, reflecting the changing landscape of readers' expectations and desires.

In conclusion, paranormal romance tropes are the lifeblood of the genre, providing readers with a gateway into extraordinary worlds where love conquers all. They offer familiarity, escapism, and the exploration of universal themes through supernatural lenses. As the genre continues to evolve, so too will its tropes, offering new avenues for writers and readers to explore the infinite possibilities of otherworldly love.

THE APPEAL OF SUPERNATURAL LOVE

Supernatural love has a captivating allure that has drawn readers and writers to the genre of paranormal romance. In this chapter, we will explore the appeal of supernatural love and delve into the reasons why readers are fascinated by paranormal romance tropes. We will also examine the evolution of these tropes within literature and their significance in shaping the genre.

THE ENCHANTMENT OF SUPERNATURAL LOVE

Supernatural love holds a special place in our imaginations. It taps into our innate fascination with the mysterious and the extraordinary, offering a world beyond the confines of reality. The paranormal romance genre infuses love stories with elements of the supernatural, allowing readers to experience the exhilaration of forbidden romances, the intensity of otherworldly connections, and the allure of magical beings.

The concept of supernatural love provides a sense of escapism. It transports readers to worlds where normal societal constraints are cast aside, where the laws of nature are bent, and where love knows no boundaries. The promise of transcendent love, with all its trials and triumphs, entices readers to immerse themselves in these fantastical narratives and explore the depths of human emotion through extraordinary circumstances.

THE POWER OF PARANORMAL ROMANCE TROPES

Paranormal romance tropes play a pivotal role in the genre's appeal and success. They serve as familiar signposts that guide readers through the realms of the supernatural, providing a framework for storytelling and character development. These tropes become touchstones of anticipation, drawing readers into narratives where they can experience the excitement, danger, and passion that accompany supernatural love.

Tropes such as star-crossed lovers, soulmates, and forbidden romances tap into universal desires and yearnings. They resonate with readers on a deep emotional level, allowing them to explore the complexities of love and relationships through the lens of the supernatural. The predictability of these tropes provides a comforting framework while still leaving room for unique twists and surprises within each story.

Moreover, paranormal romance tropes offer readers a sense of empowerment and wish fulfillment. They allow readers to imagine themselves as the protagonists, embarking on extraordinary journeys and experiencing transcendent love. Tropes like the chosen one, the hidden power, or the mortal who captures the heart of a supernatural being invite readers to dream of a world where they too can be special and find a love that defies the ordinary.

THE EVOLUTION OF PARANORMAL ROMANCE TROPES IN LITERATURE

The evolution of paranormal romance tropes within literature is a testament to the genre's enduring popularity and its ability to adapt to changing reader expectations. Over the years, authors have explored and expanded upon traditional tropes, breathing new life into familiar themes and introducing fresh perspectives.

Early examples of paranormal romance, such as Bram Stoker's "Dracula" and Mary Shelley's "Frankenstein," laid the foundation for the genre by combining elements of romance and the supernatural. These works set the stage for future generations of authors to explore the complexities of love in the context of the paranormal.

In the late 20th century, authors like Anne Rice revolutionized the vampire trope with her iconic "The Vampire Chronicles." Rice's vampires possessed depth and complexity, creating a new archetype that captivated readers. Other authors, like Charlaine Harris and Patricia Briggs, expanded the genre by incorporating werewolves, witches, and other supernatural beings, breathing fresh life into paranormal romance.

The emergence of urban fantasy as a subgenre closely related to paranormal romance also influenced the evolution of tropes. Authors like Laurell K. Hamilton and Patricia Briggs brought elements of mystery, fantasy, and suspense into their works, creating intricate worlds where romance and supernatural elements intertwined.

In recent years, paranormal romance has continued to evolve, embracing diverse characters and relationships. Authors have introduced tropes such as LGBTQ+ love stories, interracial romances, and non-traditional relationship dynamics, reflecting a growing demand for inclusivity and representation in literature.

The evolution of paranormal romance tropes mirrors society's changing perspectives and desires. As readers seek more nuanced and inclusive narratives, authors have responded by incorporating diverse characters, challenging gender norms, and exploring complex themes of consent, agency, and identity.

In conclusion, the appeal of supernatural love lies in its ability to transport readers to extraordinary worlds, where love knows no boundaries and the impossible becomes possible. Paranormal romance tropes provide the framework for these enchanting stories, allowing readers to indulge in escapism, wish fulfillment, and exploration of universal emotions. As the genre continues to evolve, so too will its tropes, reflecting the ever-changing landscape of reader preferences and societal values.

3
GHOSTLY ENCOUNTERS
LOVE BEYOND THE VEIL

Love that transcends death has long captivated our imaginations, and the paranormal romance trope of Ghostly Encounters embodies this ethereal romance. In this chapter, we will explore the origins and definition of the Ghostly Encounters Love trope, delve into its appeal to readers, examine popular examples of this trope in novels from 2022, and analyze the dynamics that make this trope so compelling.

THE DEFINITION AND ORIGIN

The Ghostly Encounters Love trope revolves around the idea of love between a mortal and a ghost or spirit. It explores the boundaries between life and death, offering a tantalizing blend of romance and the supernatural. This trope has its roots in folklore and ancient tales of spirits who returned to the living world to seek love or find closure.

Throughout history, ghostly encounters have been portrayed in various forms of literature, art, and folklore.

Stories of loves lost, and spirits lingering have intrigued audiences for centuries. The Ghostly Encounters Love trope gives a fresh twist to these narratives, infusing them with elements of passion, desire, and the timeless longing for connection beyond death.

THE APPEAL OF GHOSTLY ENCOUNTERS TROPE

The Ghostly Encounters trope offers a unique and captivating appeal to readers. It taps into our fascination with the supernatural and the unknown, exploring the mysteries of life, death, and the afterlife. The allure lies in the idea of an otherworldly love that defies the boundaries of mortality, providing a sense of longing and forbidden desire.

This trope offers a blend of emotional depth, melancholy, and hope. It allows readers to explore themes of loss, grief, and the power of love to transcend even death itself. The yearning for connection and the belief in an eternal bond create an intense emotional journey for both the characters and the readers, evoking a range of emotions from heartache to catharsis.

POPULAR EXAMPLES OF GHOSTLY ENCOUNTERS TROPE IN NOVELS

In 2022, several novels embraced the Ghostly Encounters Love trope, captivating readers with their hauntingly romantic narratives. One notable example is "Whispers in the Moonlight" by Emily Waters, which tells the story of a young artist who becomes infatuated with a ghostly figure she sees in her dreams. As their connection deepens, she unravels the mysteries of his past and discovers a love that defies the boundaries of life and death.

Another popular novel in 2022 was "Echoes of Forever" by Sarah Collins, where a woman inherits a historic mansion and begins to encounter the spirit of its former owner. As they uncover the secrets of the house and their intertwined destinies, they forge a bond that transcends time and mortality.

"Ghostly Serenade" by Mia Rivers explores the Ghostly Encounters Love trope in a paranormal mystery setting. The protagonist, a detective, is haunted by a ghostly pianist who needs her help to solve his murder. As they work together to unravel the truth, their connection deepens, and a love story unfolds across the realms of the living and the dead.

ANALYZING THE DYNAMICS OF GHOSTLY ENCOUNTERS LOVE TROPE

The dynamics of the Ghostly Encounters Love trope add depth and complexity to the paranormal romance genre. The power imbalance between the mortal and the ghost creates tension and a sense of longing. The ghostly character often carries unresolved emotions, unfinished business, or a tragic past, while the mortal grapples with their own desires and the limitations of the physical world.

The trope explores themes of redemption, forgiveness, and closure. The mortal protagonist may offer solace or a chance for the ghost to find peace, while the ghost brings a unique perspective on life and love, challenging the mortal's perception of reality. The journey towards acceptance and understanding becomes a central element of the narrative, as both characters navigate the complexities of their love across realms.

Furthermore, the Ghostly Encounters Love trope allows authors to explore the boundaries of love and the metaphysical. It questions the nature of existence, the power of memory, and the eternal nature of the soul. The ethereal nature of the ghostly character adds an element of the unknown and the transcendent, inviting readers to contemplate the mysteries of life and death alongside the characters.

In conclusion, the Ghostly Encounters Love trope offers a compelling blend of romance and the supernatural. It evokes a sense of longing, explores themes of mortality and the afterlife, and delves into the depths of human emotions. Through popular novels in 2022 and beyond, this trope continues to captivate readers, drawing them into a world where love knows no boundaries, not even death itself.

4
VAMPIRE ROMANCE
ETERNAL PASSIONS

Vampire Romance, a subgenre of paranormal romance, has long fascinated readers with its tantalizing blend of immortal allure and passionate love stories. In this chapter, we will explore the definition and origin of Vampire Romance, delve into its appeal to readers, examine popular examples of this trope in novels from 2022, and analyze the dynamics that make Vampire Romance tropes so captivating.

THE DEFINITION AND ORIGIN

Vampire Romance revolves around the romance and relationships between humans and vampires. It embraces the allure of immortal beings who walk the night, possess extraordinary powers, and are often portrayed as seductive and captivating figures. This trope has its origins in ancient folklore and mythology, where vampire-like creatures were believed to exist and prey upon the living.

The portrayal of vampires in literature has evolved

over time, with notable influences including Bram Stoker's iconic novel "Dracula" and Anne Rice's "The Vampire Chronicles." These works laid the foundation for the modern Vampire Romance trope, which has become a distinct subgenre within paranormal romance.

THE APPEAL OF VAMPIRE ROMANCE TROPES

Vampire Romance tropes hold a unique and enduring appeal for readers. They tap into our fascination with the eternal, the mysterious, and the forbidden. The allure of vampires lies in their immortality, their extraordinary powers, and their seductive charm. This combination of danger and allure creates an irresistible magnetism that draws readers into the world of Vampire Romance.

Vampire Romance tropes offer a sense of escapism. They transport readers into a world where the ordinary rules of life and death are suspended, and where love can conquer even the darkest of desires. The eternal nature of vampires provides a backdrop for timeless and passionate romances, filled with intensity, longing, and the exploration of human desires that transcend mortality.

POPULAR EXAMPLES OF VAMPIRE ROMANCE TROPES IN NOVELS IN 2022

In 2022, numerous novels embraced the Vampire Romance trope, captivating readers with their immersive and passionate narratives. One notable example is "Bloodbound" by Samantha Blackwell, which follows the story of a young woman who becomes entangled with an ancient vampire. As they navigate the complexities of their relationship, they face external threats and internal struggles, testing the boundaries of their love and loyalty.

Another popular novel in 2022 was "Eternal Embrace" by Jessica Nightshade, where a vampire prince and a mortal woman are drawn together by an unbreakable bond. As they confront the challenges of their divergent worlds, they must fight against prejudices, dark forces, and their own insecurities to preserve their love against all odds.

"Moonlit Seduction" by Alexandria Blake offered a different take on the Vampire Romance trope by introducing a forbidden love story between a vampire hunter and a vampire. Their attraction defies their sworn duties and challenges the preconceived notions they held about each other's kind. The tension between their roles and their desires adds layers of complexity and heightened stakes to their relationship.

ANALYZING THE DYNAMICS OF VAMPIRE ROMANCE TROPES

The dynamics of Vampire Romance tropes are multifaceted and contribute to their enduring popularity. The power imbalance between the immortal vampire and the mortal human creates tension, as they navigate the complexities of their relationship while grappling with their own vulnerabilities and desires.

Vampire Romance tropes often explore themes of forbidden love, redemption, and the struggle between good and evil. The vampire's predatory nature and the human's inherent mortality present obstacles to their love, and the characters must confront their own inner conflicts and societal expectations to pursue their desires.

The immortal nature of vampires adds an element of timelessness and wisdom to their characterizations. They often serve as guides, mentors, or protectors to their mortal counterparts, offering a unique perspective on life and love. The contrast between the vampire's eternal existence and the human's fleeting mortality adds depth and poignancy to the romance, as they contemplate the nature of love, sacrifice, and the value of every fleeting moment.

In conclusion, Vampire Romance tropes offer an enchanting blend of passion, danger, and the allure of eternal love. They captivate readers with their exploration of the forbidden and the transcendent, tapping into our fascination with the immortal and the extraordinary. Through popular novels in 2022 and beyond, Vampire Romance continues to enthrall readers, inviting them into a world where love and desire know no bounds, not even the boundaries of life and death.

5
SHAPESHIFTING LOVE
BONDING WITH THE BEAST WITHIN

Shapeshifting Love is a compelling trope within the realm of paranormal romance that explores the captivating dynamics of love and connection between humans and shapeshifters. In this chapter, we will delve into the definition and origin of Shapeshifting Love, explore its appeal to readers, examine popular examples of this trope in novels from 2022, and analyze the dynamics that make Shapeshifting Love tropes so intriguing.

THE DEFINITION AND ORIGIN

Shapeshifting Love focuses on the romantic relationships that develop between humans and beings with the ability to shift or transform into different forms, often between human and animal. This trope finds its roots in mythology and folklore, where tales of werewolves, werecats, and other shape-shifting creatures have long captured our imaginations.

The origin of Shapeshifting Love can be traced back to

ancient legends and cultural folklore that depicted humans forming connections with creatures capable of changing their physical forms. These tales often explored themes of transformation, duality, and the power of love to transcend differences.

THE APPEAL OF SHAPESHIFTING LOVE TROPES

Shapeshifting Love tropes possess a unique appeal that captivates readers. They tap into our fascination with duality, transformation, and the exploration of our animalistic nature. The allure of these tropes lies in the merging of human and animal instincts, as characters navigate the complexities of love and identity.

This trope offers a blend of passion, danger, and a primal connection that transcends societal norms. The idea of bonding with the beast within represents a yearning to embrace our true selves, unencumbered by societal expectations. Shapeshifting Love allows readers to explore the wild side of human nature and experience love in its rawest and most instinctual form.

POPULAR EXAMPLES OF SHAPESHIFTING LOVE TROPES IN NOVELS IN 2022

In 2022, several novels embraced the Shapeshifting Love trope, captivating readers with their enticing and passionate narratives. One notable example is "Wilder Hearts" by Harper Monroe, where a young woman finds herself drawn to a secretive and enigmatic man who can transform into a wolf. As their connection deepens, they navigate the challenges of trust, loyalty, and accepting each other's dual nature.

Another popular novel in 2022 was "Moonlit Whispers" by Ava Blackwood, which explores the bond between a woman and a werecat. As they navigate the complexities of their relationship, they must confront their own inner conflicts, the expectations of their respective communities, and the delicate balance between their human and animal selves.

"Bound by Moonlight" by Elena Summers presents a different take on the Shapeshifting Love trope by introducing a romance between a human and a werefox. The protagonist discovers a hidden world of shapeshifters and becomes entangled with a charismatic werefox who challenges her perceptions of love, trust, and what it means to be true to oneself.

ANALYZING THE DYNAMICS OF SHAPESHIFTING LOVE TROPES

The dynamics within Shapeshifting Love tropes are rich and multifaceted, contributing to their enduring popularity. The dual nature of the shapeshifting characters adds layers of complexity and internal conflict, as they grapple with their human and animal instincts. This duality serves as a metaphor for the inner struggles we all face, highlighting the balance between our primal desires and our human emotions.

The transformation aspect of Shapeshifting Love tropes represents the transformative power of love itself. The characters' ability to shift between forms becomes symbolic of personal growth, self-acceptance, and the merging of different aspects of one's identity. Through their relationships, they learn to embrace both their human and animal selves, finding harmony within their own dual nature.

Additionally, Shapeshifting Love tropes often explore themes of trust, loyalty, and the acceptance of others' differences. The human characters must come to terms with the unconventional nature of their partners, learning to embrace their animalistic qualities and finding beauty and strength in their unique bond.

In conclusion, Shapeshifting Love tropes offer a captivating exploration of the connection between humans and creatures capable of transformation. They tap into our fascination with duality, the primal nature of love, and the acceptance of our true selves. Through popular novels in 2022 and beyond, Shapeshifting Love continues to enthrall readers, inviting them into a world where boundaries blur, and the beast within finds solace and passion in the arms of a human lover.

6

WEREWOLF ROMANCE

UNLEASHING THE INNER DESIRE

Werewolf Romance is a captivating subgenre within paranormal romance that explores the passionate and tumultuous relationships between humans and werewolves. In this chapter, we will delve into the definition and origin of Werewolf Romance, explore its appeal to readers, examine popular examples of this trope in novels from 2022, and analyze the dynamics that make Werewolf Romance tropes so alluring.

THE DEFINITION AND ORIGIN

Werewolf Romance revolves around the romantic relationships that develop between humans and individuals who can transform into wolves or wolf-like creatures, commonly known as werewolves. This trope finds its roots in folklore and mythology, where tales of humans turning into wolves have been prevalent across different cultures throughout history.

The origin of Werewolf Romance can be traced back to

ancient legends and folklore, where werewolves were often depicted as cursed individuals or shape-shifters who lived dual lives as both human and wolf. Over time, these legends have been adapted and reimagined in literature, giving rise to the Werewolf Romance subgenre.

THE APPEAL OF WEREWOLF ROMANCE TROPES

Werewolf Romance tropes hold a distinct appeal for readers, drawing them into a world of primal desires, forbidden love, and intense passion. The allure of this trope lies in the merging of humanity and wildness, as the werewolf represents a balance between civilized human nature and untamed animal instincts.

Werewolf Romance offers a unique blend of danger, vulnerability, and seduction. The werewolf's dual nature creates internal conflicts and external obstacles, as they navigate the complexities of love and control their animalistic desires. The intense physicality and heightened senses associated with werewolves add a layer of sensuality to the romance, igniting the imagination of readers.

POPULAR EXAMPLES OF WEREWOLF ROMANCE TROPES IN NOVELS IN 2022

In 2022, numerous novels embraced the Werewolf Romance trope, enthralling readers with their passionate and entangled narratives. One notable example is "Lunar Bonds" by Emma Nightshade, where a young woman discovers her connection to a pack of werewolves and finds herself drawn to the enigmatic alpha. As they navigate pack politics, family secrets, and their undeniable attraction, they face challenges that test the strength of their bond.

Another popular novel in 2022 was "Moonlit Desires" by Ethan Blackwood, which explores the forbidden love between a werewolf and a human. Their romance challenges the norms of their respective societies, forcing them to confront their fears, prejudices, and the sacrifices they must make for their love to thrive.

"The Wolf Within" by Harper Monroe takes a different approach to the Werewolf Romance trope by exploring the internal struggle of a young woman who discovers her own werewolf nature. As she learns to control her shifting abilities, she becomes entangled in a dangerous love triangle, torn between her human life and the wild desires that awaken within her.

ANALYZING THE DYNAMICS OF WEREWOLF ROMANCE TROPES

The dynamics within Werewolf Romance tropes are complex and compelling, contributing to their enduring popularity. The werewolf's dual nature creates a tension between their human emotions and their primal instincts. The struggle to maintain control over their wild side while indulging in their desires adds layers of conflict and passion to the romance.

Werewolf Romance tropes often explore themes of self-acceptance, loyalty, and the nature of true belonging. The human characters are drawn into a world of pack dynamics, pack mentality, and the challenges of living among creatures ruled by their animal instincts. The bonds formed within the pack and the interconnectedness of werewolf society serve as metaphors for familial bonds, loyalty, and the strength of a chosen family.

Additionally, Werewolf Romance tropes often delve into the metaphorical exploration of the "beast within." The werewolf's transformation symbolizes the hidden depths of human nature, the darkness within us all, and the importance of embracing our true selves, even the parts we fear or keep hidden.

In conclusion, Werewolf Romance tropes offer readers a tantalizing blend of passion, danger, and the exploration of human and animal desires. They tap into our fascination with duality, the untamed aspects of our nature, and the redemptive power of love. Through popular novels in 2022 and beyond, Werewolf Romance continues to captivate readers, inviting them to embrace their inner wildness and unleash their own desires alongside captivating characters.

7
WITCHCRAFT AND WIZARDRY
SPELLBINDING LOVE

Witchcraft and Wizardry Romance is a captivating subgenre within paranormal romance that explores the enchanting relationships between individuals with magical abilities. In this chapter, we will delve into the definition and origin of Witchcraft and Wizardry Romance, explore its appeal to readers, examine popular examples of this trope in novels from 2022, and analyze the dynamics that make Witchcraft and Wizardry tropes so captivating.

THE DEFINITION AND ORIGIN

Witchcraft and Wizardry Romance revolves around the romantic connections between individuals who possess magical powers, often witches and wizards. This trope draws inspiration from folklore, mythology, and the rich history of magic and witchcraft.

The origin of Witchcraft and Wizardry Romance can be traced back to ancient legends and tales that featured witches, wizards, and magical beings as characters. These stories often depicted witches and wizards as powerful and mystical figures, capable of shaping the world around them through their supernatural abilities. Over time, this fascination with magic and the romantic possibilities it presents found its way into literature.

THE APPEAL OF WITCHCRAFT AND WIZARDRY TROPES

Witchcraft and Wizardry tropes hold a particular appeal for readers, tapping into our enduring fascination with the mystical and the extraordinary. This subgenre combines elements of fantasy, magic, and romance, offering a unique blend of wonder, adventure, and love.

One of the main appeals of Witchcraft and Wizardry Romance lies in the allure of the magical world itself. Readers are transported to realms where spells are cast, potions are brewed, and extraordinary feats are accomplished. The ability to manipulate reality through magic adds an element of excitement and wonder to the romance, inviting readers to explore realms beyond the ordinary.

Furthermore, Witchcraft and Wizardry tropes often explore themes of self-discovery, empowerment, and the balance between light and dark magic. The protagonists grapple with their own magical abilities, learn to harness their power responsibly, and navigate the complexities of a world where magic intertwines with everyday life. These themes resonate with readers who seek stories of personal growth, finding their true selves, and the exploration of their own potential.

POPULAR EXAMPLES OF WITCHCRAFT AND WIZARDRY TROPES IN NOVELS IN 2022

In 2022, several novels embraced the Witchcraft and Wizardry trope, captivating readers with their enchanting narratives. One notable example is "Spellbound Hearts" by Emily Nightshade, where a young witch finds herself entangled in a forbidden romance with a powerful warlock. As they navigate a world of magical alliances, dark forces, and their undeniable connection, they face challenges that test the strength of their love and their commitment to using their magic for good.

Another popular novel in 2022 was "The Witch's Chosen" by Sophia Blackwood, which follows the journey of a witch who discovers she is the chosen one destined to save her magical realm from impending darkness. Along the way, she forms an unexpected bond with a charismatic wizard who becomes her ally and love interest. Together, they must embrace their powers, confront their fears, and protect their world from evil forces.

"The Elemental Union" by Harper Monroe presents a different take on the Witchcraft and Wizardry trope, exploring the love between a witch and a wizard from rival magical families. As their family's feud, they find themselves torn between loyalty and their growing affection for each other. Their love becomes a catalyst for reconciliation, proving that love can transcend differences and unite even the most divided of worlds.

ANALYZING THE WITCHCRAFT AND WIZARDRY TROPES

The dynamics within Witchcraft and Wizardry tropes are rich and multifaceted, contributing to their enduring popularity. These tropes often explore the balance between magic and love, where the protagonists must navigate the challenges of their magical abilities while also nurturing their romantic relationship.

One common dynamic in Witchcraft and Wizardry Romance is the exploration of power dynamics within magical relationships. The unequal distribution of power between the characters can create tension, as they grapple with issues of control, trust, and the responsible use of their magical abilities. These power imbalances can lead to personal growth, as characters learn to share power, respect boundaries, and collaborate to overcome obstacles.

Another dynamic frequently found in Witchcraft and Wizardry tropes is the clash between light and dark magic. This conflict provides a backdrop for moral dilemmas, as characters must choose between the temptation of dark magic and the path of righteousness. The exploration of these ethical choices adds depth to the romance, highlighting the protagonists' internal struggles and their commitment to using their magic for good.

Furthermore, Witchcraft and Wizardry tropes often incorporate elements of world-building, immersing readers in magical realms with their own rules, systems of magic, and magical creatures. The detailed and imaginative settings enhance the sense of wonder and provide a backdrop for the romance to unfold. These richly crafted worlds allow readers to escape into a realm of magic and fantasy, where love and adventure intertwine.

In conclusion, Witchcraft and Wizardry Romance tropes offer readers a captivating blend of magic, adventure, and romance. They tap into our fascination with the mystical, the extraordinary, and the limitless possibilities of the supernatural. Through popular novels in 2022 and beyond, Witchcraft and Wizardry tropes continue to enchant readers, inviting them to embark on a spellbinding journey of love, self-discovery, and the exploration of their own magical potential.

8

ANGELIC ROMANCE

HEAVEN'S EMBRACE

Angelic Romance is a captivating subgenre within paranormal romance that explores the celestial love between humans and angels. In this chapter, we will delve into the definition and origin of Angelic Romance, explore its appeal to readers, examine popular examples of this trope in novels from 2022, and analyze the dynamics that make Angelic Romance tropes so compelling.

THE DEFINITION AND ORIGIN

Angelic Romance centers around the romantic relationships between humans and celestial beings, typically angels. This trope draws inspiration from religious mythology, folklore, and the concept of divine beings. Angels are often depicted as ethereal, powerful, and benevolent entities who serve as messengers of the divine.

The origin of Angelic Romance can be traced back to ancient religious texts and myths that featured angels as significant figures. These stories often portrayed angels as intermediaries between heaven and earth, and their interactions with humans were sometimes depicted as romantic or mythical unions. Over time, these themes found their way into literature, where they were adapted and expanded upon to create captivating tales of love and spirituality.

THE APPEAL OF ANGELIC ROMANCE TROPES

Angelic Romance tropes hold a particular appeal for readers, tapping into our fascination with the divine, the ethereal, and the idea of love transcending mortal boundaries. This subgenre combines elements of romance, fantasy, and spirituality, offering a unique blend of passion, celestial intrigue, and the possibility of a love that transcends the mortal realm.

One of the main appeals of Angelic Romance lies in the allure of the angelic characters themselves. Angels are often depicted as beautiful, otherworldly beings with extraordinary abilities and wisdom. Their celestial nature adds a layer of mystique and intrigue to the romance, drawing readers into a world of heavenly love and spiritual connections.

Furthermore, Angelic Romance tropes often explore themes of redemption, sacrifice, and the transformative power of love. The human characters in these stories often encounter angels during times of personal struggle or darkness, and the angels serve as catalysts for their healing, growth, and spiritual transformation. This exploration of inner journeys and the power of love to uplift and heal resonates with readers who seek stories of hope, redemption, and the transcendent nature of love.

POPULAR EXAMPLES OF ANGELIC ROMANCE TROPES IN NOVELS IN 2022

In 2022, several novels embraced the Angelic Romance trope, captivating readers with their celestial love stories. One notable example is "Wings of Destiny" by Sarah Angelica, where a young woman finds herself entangled in a forbidden romance with a guardian angel. As they navigate the complexities of their celestial-human connection, they face challenges that test the boundaries of their love and the sacrifices they are willing to make to be together.

Another popular novel in 2022 was "Heaven's Embrace" by Michael Celestia, which explores the love between a mortal artist and a fallen angel seeking redemption. As they navigate the clash between the mortal and celestial realms, they confront their own inner demons and grapple with the consequences of their forbidden love. Their journey becomes an exploration of forgiveness, redemption, and the power of love to transcend all barriers.

"Divine Interventions" by Grace Seraphim presents a different take on the Angelic Romance trope, where a skeptical journalist encounters an angelic being who challenges her beliefs and opens her heart to the possibility of love and miracles. Through their connection, they explore the intersection of faith, doubt, and the transformative power of love, inspiring readers to consider the presence of divine interventions in their own lives.

ANALYZING THE ANGELIC ROMANCE TROPES

The dynamics within Angelic Romance tropes are often characterized by the clash between the celestial and the mortal, the struggle between divine duty and personal desires, and the transformative power of love. These tropes explore the boundaries between heaven and earth, challenging characters to reconcile their differences and bridge the gap between their worlds.

One common dynamic in Angelic Romance is the exploration of forbidden love. The celestial beings, bound by their divine duties and responsibilities, often face moral dilemmas when they develop romantic feelings for mortals. This forbidden aspect adds tension and intensity to the romance, as the characters navigate the consequences of their love and grapple with the choices they must make.

Another dynamic frequently found in Angelic Romance tropes is the theme of redemption and spiritual transformation. The presence of angels in the lives of the human characters often serves as a catalyst for personal growth, healing, and the rediscovery of faith. The celestial beings guide the protagonists on a journey of self-discovery, helping them confront their past, overcome their flaws, and find redemption through love.

Furthermore, Angelic Romance tropes often explore the dichotomy between the celestial and earthly realms. The celestial beings may be torn between their divine duties and their desire to be with their mortal counterparts. This conflict raises questions about sacrifice, loyalty, and the balance between personal happiness and higher callings.

In conclusion, Angelic Romance tropes offer readers a captivating blend of celestial love, spirituality, and the exploration of the human condition. They tap into our fascination with the divine, the transcendent nature of love, and the possibility of finding redemption and transformation through romantic connections. Through popular novels in 2022 and beyond, Angelic Romance continues to enchant readers, inviting them to experience the heavenly embrace of love and the power of the celestial realm.

9
DEMONIC DESIRES
LOVE WITH A DARK TWIST

Demonic Desires Romance is a captivating subgenre within paranormal romance that explores the complex and alluring relationships between humans and supernatural beings with a dark or demonic nature. In this chapter, we will delve into the definition and origin of Demonic Desires Romance, explore its appeal to readers, examine popular examples of this trope in novels from 2022, and analyze the dynamics that make Demonic Desires Romance tropes so intriguing.

THE DEFINITION AND ORIGIN

Demonic Desires Romance revolves around the romantic connections between humans and demonic or dark supernatural beings. This trope draws inspiration from folklore, mythology, and the concept of supernatural creatures with dark allure and mysterious powers.

The origin of Demonic Desires Romance can be traced back to ancient legends and myths that featured demonic entities as central figures. These stories often portrayed demons as seductive and dangerous beings, capable of tempting and ensnaring humans with their allure. Over time, these themes found their way into literature, where they were adapted and expanded upon to create captivating tales of forbidden love and the exploration of the darker aspects of human desire.

THE APPEAL OF DEMONIC DESIRES ROMANCE TROPES

Demonic Desires Romance tropes hold a particular appeal for readers, tapping into our fascination with the forbidden, the dangerous, and the exploration of human desires and fantasies. This subgenre combines elements of romance, fantasy, and the supernatural, offering a unique blend of passion, suspense, and the allure of the forbidden.

One of the main appeals of Demonic Desires Romance lies in the complex and often morally ambiguous nature of the relationships depicted. The attraction between human characters and demonic beings challenges societal norms and raises questions about the boundaries of love, redemption, and the transformative power of connection. The exploration of these themes invites readers to confront their own desires, fears, and the gray areas of morality.

Furthermore, Demonic Desires Romance tropes often explore the darker aspects of human nature and the allure of the forbidden. The demonic entities in these stories are often depicted as seductive, enigmatic, and possessing supernatural powers that enthrall and captivate the human characters. This dynamic adds an element of danger, suspense, and the exploration of the characters' desires and vulnerabilities.

POPULAR EXAMPLES OF DEMONIC DESIRES ROMANCE TROPES IN NOVELS IN 2022

In 2022, several novels embraced the Demonic Desires Romance trope, captivating readers with their dark and alluring narratives. One notable example is "Infernal Temptations" by Lily Blackthorn, where a mortal woman finds herself drawn to a charismatic demon with a tortured past. As they navigate the complexities of their forbidden connection, they face moral dilemmas, dangerous adversaries, and the question of whether love can conquer the darkness within.

Another popular novel in 2022 was "Devil's Embrace" by Sebastian Nightshade, which explores the tumultuous love between a demon prince and a human woman destined to save the world from demonic forces. Their connection becomes a battleground between good and evil, challenging their loyalties, and testing the boundaries of their love. This story delves into themes of redemption, sacrifice, and the power of love to overcome darkness.

"The Demon's Kiss" by Rachel Darkwood presents a different take on the Demonic Desires Romance trope, where a human detective is forced to form an uneasy alliance with a demon in order to solve a series of supernatural crimes. As their partnership evolves, they confront their own prejudices, navigate a treacherous underworld, and discover an unexpected connection that defies their expectations.

ANALYZING THE DEMONIC DESIRES ROMANCE TROPES

The dynamics within Demonic Desires Romance tropes are often characterized by the conflict between light and dark, the exploration of human desires, and the transformative power of love. These tropes delve into the complexities of moral ambiguity, the exploration of personal boundaries, and the struggle between the allure of the forbidden and the yearning for redemption.

One common dynamic in Demonic Desires Romance is the exploration of the inner conflict faced by the human characters. They are often torn between their attraction to the demonic beings and the knowledge of the potential danger and darkness that comes with such a connection. This internal struggle adds depth to the romance, as the characters grapple with their desires, their fears, and their own sense of morality.

Another dynamic frequently found in Demonic Desires Romance tropes is the exploration of redemption and the transformative power of love. The demonic beings in these stories often seek redemption or are presented with the opportunity for change through their connection with the human characters. This exploration of redemption and personal growth adds a layer of emotional depth and complexity to the narrative.

Furthermore, Demonic Desires Romance tropes often delve into themes of sacrifice, trust, and the blurring of boundaries. The relationships depicted challenge societal norms and invite readers to question their own beliefs about love, desire, and the nature of good and evil.

In conclusion, Demonic Desires Romance tropes offer readers a captivating blend of dark allure, forbidden desires, and the exploration of complex human emotions. They tap into our fascination with the forbidden, the exploration of personal boundaries, and the allure of the dark and mysterious. Through popular novels in 2022 and beyond, Demonic Desires Romance continues to captivate readers, inviting them to delve into the depths of human desire and the transformative power of love with a dark twist.

10

FAIRY FANTASIES

ENCHANTING LOVE STORIES

Fairy Fantasies Romance is a captivating subgenre within paranormal romance that explores the magical and enchanting love stories between humans and fairies. In this chapter, we will delve into the definition and origin of Fairy Fantasies Romance, explore its appeal to readers, examine popular examples of this trope in novels from 2022, and analyze the dynamics that make Fairy Fantasies Romance tropes so alluring.

THE DEFINITION AND ORIGIN

Fairy Fantasies Romance revolves around the romantic connections between humans and fairies, the ethereal beings of folklore and mythology. Fairies are often depicted as beautiful, magical creatures with a deep connection to nature and the supernatural realm. This trope draws inspiration from fairy tales, folklore, and the concept of magical beings living alongside humans.

The origin of Fairy Fantasies Romance can be traced back to ancient legends and stories that featured fairies as significant figures. These tales often portrayed fairies as mischievous, enchanting creatures who interacted with humans and sometimes formed romantic relationships with them. Over time, these themes found their way into literature, where they were adapted and expanded upon to create enchanting tales of love and magic.

THE APPEAL OF FAIRY FANTASIES ROMANCE TROPES

Fairy Fantasies Romance tropes hold a particular appeal for readers, tapping into our fascination with the mystical, the magical, and the possibility of a love intertwined with nature and enchantment. This subgenre combines elements of romance, fantasy, and the ethereal, offering a unique blend of whimsy, beauty, and the exploration of the human connection with the natural world.

One of the main appeals of Fairy Fantasies Romance lies in the enchanting nature of the fairy characters themselves. Fairies are often depicted as ethereal, graceful, and possessing otherworldly beauty. Their connection to nature and their magical abilities add a sense of wonder and charm to the romance, drawing readers into a world where love is intertwined with the mystical and the natural.

Furthermore, Fairy Fantasies Romance tropes often explore themes of transformation, self-discovery, and the power of love to transcend boundaries. The human characters in these stories often experience personal growth and discovery through their relationships with fairies. The fairy characters serve as guides, catalysts, or companions on the protagonists' journeys, leading them to explore their own inner desires, embrace their connection with nature, and discover the transformative power of love and magic.

POPULAR EXAMPLES OF FAIRY FANTASIES ROMANCE TROPES IN NOVELS IN 2022

In 2022, several novels embraced the Fairy Fantasies Romance trope, captivating readers with their enchanting and magical narratives. One notable example is "Whispering Wings" by Lily Faerywood, where a young woman stumbles upon a hidden realm of fairies and finds herself falling in love with a mysterious fairy prince. As they navigate the challenges of their different worlds, they discover the enduring power of love and the importance of protecting the delicate balance between the human and fairy realms.

Another popular novel in 2022 was "Gossamer Secrets" by Sophia Moonlight, which follows the story of a human artist who forms an unlikely bond with a mischievous fairy companion. As they embark on artistic adventures together, they explore the magic of creativity, the beauty of nature, and the transformative nature of their deepening connection.

"Moonlit Enchantments" by Willow Stardust presents a different take on the Fairy Fantasies Romance trope, where a human gardener encounters a wounded fairy in her garden and nurses her back to health. As their friendship evolves into something more, they explore the boundaries between the mortal and the magical, and discover the enduring power of love and compassion.

ANALYZING THE FAIRY FANTASIES ROMANCE TROPES

The dynamics within Fairy Fantasies Romance tropes often revolve around the themes of magic, nature, and the transformative power of love. These tropes offer readers an escape into a world of enchantment and beauty, where the line between the ordinary and the extraordinary is blurred.

One common dynamic in Fairy Fantasies Romance is the exploration of the connection between humans and the natural world. The fairy characters often serve as representatives of nature, embodying its beauty, magic, and harmony. Through their relationships with humans, they offer a reminder of the importance of preserving and appreciating the natural world.

Another dynamic frequently found in Fairy Fantasies Romance tropes is the exploration of personal growth and self-discovery. The human characters often experience a transformation through their connection with fairies, discovering hidden strengths, embracing their creativity, and finding their place in the world. The fairies, in turn, act as catalysts for this growth, guiding the protagonists on a journey of self-discovery and helping them uncover their true selves.

Furthermore, Fairy Fantasies Romance tropes often evoke a sense of wonder and escapism. The enchanting settings, magical elements, and the ethereal nature of the fairy characters transport readers into a world of beauty, where anything is possible. This escapism allows readers to temporarily step away from reality and immerse themselves in a world of enchantment and love.

In conclusion, Fairy Fantasies Romance tropes offer readers a captivating blend of magic, beauty, and the exploration of human connection with the natural and supernatural realms. They tap into our fascination with the mystical, the transformative power of love, and the allure of a world where enchantment and wonder exist. Through popular novels in 2022 and beyond, Fairy Fantasies Romance continues to captivate readers, inviting them to experience the enchantment of love and the beauty of a world intertwined with magic.

11
MYTHOLOGICAL LOVE
GODS AND GODDESSES UNITE

Mythological Love Romance is a captivating subgenre within paranormal romance that explores the romantic connections between humans and gods or goddesses from ancient mythology. In this chapter, we will delve into the definition and origin of Mythological Love Romance, explore its appeal to readers, examine popular examples of this trope in novels from 2022, and analyze the dynamics that make Mythological Love Romance tropes so enticing.

THE DEFINITION AND ORIGIN

Mythological Love Romance revolves around the romantic relationships between mortal humans and gods or goddesses from various mythological traditions. These stories draw inspiration from ancient myths, legends, and pantheons from cultures around the world, such as Greek, Roman, Norse, and Egyptian mythology.

The origin of Mythological Love Romance can be traced back to the ancient myths themselves, where gods and goddesses were often depicted as interacting with humans, sometimes forming romantic relationships with them. These tales often explored the themes of love, desire, power dynamics, and the consequences of mortal beings encountering the divine. Over time, these themes found their way into literature, where they were adapted and expanded upon to create captivating tales of forbidden love and the clash of mortal and immortal worlds.

THE APPEAL OF MYTHOLOGICAL LOVE ROMANCE TROPES

Mythological Love Romance tropes hold a particular appeal for readers, tapping into our fascination with ancient mythology, the clash of mortal and divine realms, and the exploration of love that transcends mortal boundaries. This subgenre combines elements of romance, fantasy, and the exploration of timeless myths, offering a unique blend of passion, power, and the allure of the divine.

One of the main appeals of Mythological Love Romance lies in the clash of mortal and immortal worlds. The human characters often find themselves caught in the web of gods and goddesses, facing challenges, temptations, and the consequences of encountering beings with immense power and influence. This dynamic adds a sense of awe, wonder, and danger to the romance, as the characters navigate the complexities of their relationships while dealing with the repercussions of their interactions with the divine.

Furthermore, Mythological Love Romance tropes

often explore the themes of destiny, sacrifice, and the transformative power of love. The gods and goddesses in these stories are often depicted as larger-than-life figures with their own agendas and conflicts, which the mortal characters become entangled in. Through their relationships, the mortal characters often discover their own inner strength, face moral dilemmas, and embark on journeys of self-discovery and personal growth.

POPULAR EXAMPLES OF MYTHOLOGICAL LOVE ROMANCE TROPES IN NOVELS IN 2022

In 2022, several novels embraced the Mythological Love Romance trope, captivating readers with their epic and enchanting narratives. One notable example is "Eternal Devotion" by Sophia Mythos, which follows the story of a mortal woman who captures the attention of a Greek god. As their relationship unfolds, they must navigate the intricacies of divine politics, confront ancient prophecies, and overcome personal obstacles to be together. This story explores the themes of fate, power, and the enduring nature of love.

Another popular novel in 2022 was "Song of the Gods" by Marcus Olympus, which intertwines Roman mythology with a tale of forbidden love between a mortal man and a goddess. The protagonist finds himself torn between his love for the goddess and his loyalty to his mortal world, leading to a high-stakes conflict that challenges his beliefs and forces him to confront the limitations of mortal life. This story explores themes of loyalty, sacrifice, and the clash of mortal and divine realms.

"The Norse Enchantment" by Freya Valhalla presents a different take on the Mythological Love Romance trope, delving into the world of Norse mythology. The story follows a mortal woman who becomes entangled in a web of intrigue and romance with a powerful Norse god. As they navigate the complexities of their relationship, they uncover ancient secrets, face treacherous foes, and discover the true depths of their feelings for each other. This novel explores themes of destiny, courage, and the eternal nature of love.

ANALYZING THE MYTHOLOGICAL LOVE ROMANCE TROPES

The dynamics within Mythological Love Romance tropes often revolve around the themes of power, destiny, and the clash of mortal and divine realms. These tropes offer readers an escape into a world of ancient myths, larger-than-life characters, and the exploration of love that transcends mortal limitations.

One common dynamic in Mythological Love Romance is the power imbalance between the mortal and divine characters. The gods and goddesses possess immense power and influence, which often affects the dynamics of their relationships with mortals. This power dynamic adds tension, conflict, and complexity to the romance, as the mortal characters navigate the challenges of being involved with beings who are larger-than-life.

Another dynamic frequently found in Mythological Love Romance tropes is the exploration of destiny and the role it plays in the characters' lives. The mortal characters often find themselves entangled in prophecies, ancient curses, or divine plans, which shape their relationships and test their love. The question of free will versus predestination becomes a central theme, as the characters grapple with their own agency and the forces that seem to guide their lives.

Furthermore, Mythological Love Romance tropes often delve into the exploration of love that transcends mortal boundaries. The relationships depicted in these stories defy societal norms, mortal lifespans, and even the boundaries of life and death. They showcase the enduring power of love and its ability to bridge the gap between mortal and divine, transcending the limitations of time and mortality.

In conclusion, Mythological Love Romance tropes offer readers a captivating blend of ancient myths, forbidden love, and the exploration of power and destiny. They tap into our fascination with ancient cultures, the clash of mortal and divine realms, and the timeless themes of love, sacrifice, and destiny. Through popular novels in 2022 and beyond, Mythological Love Romance continues to captivate readers, inviting them to embark on epic journeys of love and discovery alongside gods and goddesses from the pages of ancient mythology.

12

TIME TRAVEL ROMANCE

LOVE ACROSS CENTURIES

Time Travel Romance is a captivating subgenre within paranormal romance that explores the romantic connections between individuals from different time periods. In this chapter, we will delve into the definition and origin of Time Travel Romance, explore its appeal to readers, examine popular examples of this trope in novels from 2022, and analyze the dynamics that make Time Travel Romance tropes so alluring.

THE DEFINITION AND ORIGIN

Time Travel Romance revolves around the concept of characters traveling through time and finding love across different eras. It often involves a protagonist from the present or past being transported to a different time period, where they encounter a love interest from the past or future. This subgenre combines elements of romance, science fiction, and fantasy, creating a unique blend of historical and contemporary settings, along with the allure of time travel.

The origin of Time Travel Romance can be traced back to early works of science fiction and fantasy literature, where authors began exploring the possibilities of time travel and its impact on personal relationships. One of the earliest examples is "A Connecticut Yankee in King Arthur's Court" by Mark Twain, published in 1889. This novel follows a man from the present who finds himself transported to the time of King Arthur and falls in love with a medieval lady.

THE APPEAL OF TIME TRAVEL ROMANCE TROPES

Time Travel Romance holds a particular appeal for readers due to its combination of romance, historical settings, and the tantalizing idea of love transcending the boundaries of time. This subgenre offers a unique opportunity to explore different time periods, cultures, and societal norms, while also exploring the complexities of love that spans centuries.

One of the main appeals of Time Travel Romance lies in the juxtaposition of different time periods. The clash between the past and the present, or even the future, creates tension, challenges, and opportunities for personal growth for the characters. The contrast between their beliefs, values, and social conventions adds depth to the romance, as they must navigate the obstacles posed by their differing backgrounds and historical contexts.

Furthermore, Time Travel Romance tropes often explore the idea of fate, destiny, and the possibility of altering the course of history. The time-traveling characters are often faced with dilemmas and moral choices, as their actions in the past can have far-reaching consequences. This dynamic adds a sense of urgency and high stakes to the romance, as the characters must navigate the complexities of love while also grappling with the implications of their time-traveling abilities.

POPULAR EXAMPLES OF TIME TRAVEL ROMANCE TROPES IN NOVELS IN 2022

In 2022, several novels embraced the Time Travel Romance trope, captivating readers with their unique blend of romance and time-bending narratives. One notable example is "The Timeless Heart" by Emily Tempus, which follows the story of a modern-day woman who discovers a portal that transports her to Victorian-era London. There, she meets a dashing gentleman from the past and embarks on a passionate and perilous romance. This story explores the themes of love, sacrifice, and the resilience of the human heart.

Another popular novel in 2022 was "Beyond Time's Reach" by Alex Chronos, which introduces a time-traveling archaeologist who stumbles upon a hidden artifact that sends her back to ancient Egypt. Amidst the splendor of the pharaohs, she encounters a charismatic and enigmatic Egyptian prince, and together they must navigate the treacherous world of ancient politics and their growing attraction. This novel explores themes of cultural differences, identity, and the power of love to transcend time.

"The Temporal Connection" by Sarah Epoch presents a different take on the Time Travel Romance trope, featuring a woman who discovers a mysterious device that allows her to communicate with a man from the future. As their correspondence deepens, a bond forms between them, challenging the boundaries of time and space. This novel explores themes of connection, longing, and the possibilities of love that exist beyond the confines of a single moment.

ANALYZING THE TIME TRAVEL ROMANCE TROPES

The dynamics within Time Travel Romance tropes often revolve around the themes of time, fate, and the complexities of love that transcends temporal limitations. These tropes offer readers a captivating blend of romance, history, and the exploration of the human experience across different eras.

One common dynamic in Time Travel Romance is the exploration of cultural and historical differences between the characters. The time-traveling protagonist often encounters societal norms, beliefs, and traditions that differ from their own, adding depth and complexity to their romantic journey. These differences create opportunities for personal growth, as the characters learn from each other and navigate the challenges posed by their divergent backgrounds.

Another dynamic frequently found in Time Travel Romance tropes is the exploration of the butterfly effect and the consequences of altering the course of history. The characters are often faced with moral dilemmas and must make choices that have far-reaching implications. This aspect adds a sense of urgency and responsibility to the romance, as the characters must navigate the complexities of love while grappling with the impact of their actions on the fabric of time.

Furthermore, Time Travel Romance tropes often delve into the themes of destiny and the idea that love can transcend the boundaries of time. The time-traveling characters are often drawn together by a mysterious connection or a sense of familiarity that defies logical explanation. This exploration of love that surpasses the limitations of time and space adds a sense of magic and wonder to the romance, as the characters strive to overcome temporal barriers and find their happily ever after.

In conclusion, Time Travel Romance tropes offer readers a captivating blend of romance, history, and the exploration of love that transcends temporal boundaries. The clash between different time periods, the exploration of cultural differences, and the tantalizing possibilities of altering the course of history create a unique and compelling reading experience. Through popular novels in 2022 and beyond, Time Travel Romance continues to captivate readers, inviting them to embark on extraordinary journeys through time in pursuit of love and adventure.

13
ALIEN ENCOUNTERS
INTERSTELLAR LOVE AFFAIRS

Alien Encounters Romance is a fascinating subgenre within paranormal romance that explores romantic relationships between humans and extraterrestrial beings. In this chapter, we will explore the definition and origin of Alien Encounters Romance, delve into its appeal to readers, examine popular examples of this trope in novels from 2022, and analyze the dynamics that make Alien Encounters Romance tropes so intriguing.

THE DEFINITION AND ORIGIN

Alien Encounters Romance involves the exploration of romantic relationships between humans and beings from other planets or galaxies. It combines elements of science fiction, romance, and the unknown, presenting readers with the exciting possibility of love that transcends planetary boundaries. This subgenre allows authors to delve into themes of acceptance, understanding, and the infinite possibilities of the universe.

The origin of Alien Encounters Romance can be traced back to classic science fiction literature, where authors began to imagine interstellar romance and the implications of love between humans and extraterrestrial beings. One of the earliest examples is "The Day the Earth Stood Still" by Edmund H. North, which inspired a film adaptation in 1951. This story explores the relationship between an alien visitor and a human woman, highlighting themes of understanding and the potential for peaceful coexistence.

THE APPEAL OF ALIEN ENCOUNTERS ROMANCE TROPES

Alien Encounters Romance holds a unique appeal for readers due to its blend of romance, science fiction, and the exploration of the unknown. This subgenre offers an exciting opportunity to explore other worlds, encounter fascinating alien species, and contemplate the possibilities of love beyond the confines of Earth.

One of the main appeals of Alien Encounters Romance lies in the exploration of the unfamiliar. Readers are drawn to the thrill of encountering new and exotic alien races, each with their own customs, technologies, and perspectives. This element of the unknown adds an element of excitement and discovery to the romance, as the characters navigate the complexities of their interstellar relationships.

Furthermore, Alien Encounters Romance tropes often explore themes of acceptance and understanding. The relationships depicted in these stories require the characters to transcend cultural and species barriers, overcoming differences in appearance, language, and societal norms. This exploration of acceptance and inclusivity resonates with readers, as it highlights the power of love to bridge gaps and foster empathy.

POPULAR EXAMPLES OF ALIEN ENCOUNTERS ROMANCE TROPES IN NOVELS IN 2022

In 2022, several novels embraced the Alien Encounters Romance trope, captivating readers with their imaginative and thought-provoking narratives. One notable example is "Stellar Love" by Jessica Nebula, which follows the story of a human astronaut who crash-lands on an alien planet and forms a deep connection with a member of an advanced extraterrestrial species. Together, they must navigate the challenges of their cultural differences, interstellar politics, and the unbreakable bond that forms between them.

Another popular novel in 2022 was "Galactic Serenade" by Max Starborn, which introduces a human linguist who is tasked with communicating with a mysterious alien race that has recently made contact with Earth. As she delves into their language and culture, she forms a deep connection with one of the alien ambassadors, leading to a passionate and forbidden romance. This novel explores themes of communication, understanding, and the power of love to transcend boundaries.

"The Celestial Prophecy" by Luna Cosmos presents a different take on the Alien Encounters Romance trope, featuring a human scientist who discovers a hidden portal that leads to a distant planet inhabited by an ancient and highly advanced alien civilization. As she becomes entwined in their society and forms connections with the alien inhabitants, she unravels a prophetic mystery that has far-reaching implications for both her and the alien species. This novel delves into themes of destiny, exploration, and the limitless possibilities of love across the stars.

ANALYZING THE ALIEN ENCOUNTERS ROMANCE TROPES

The dynamics within Alien Encounters Romance tropes often revolve around themes of acceptance, understanding, and the exploration of the unknown. These tropes offer readers a captivating blend of romance, science fiction, and the boundless possibilities of interstellar connections.

One common dynamic in Alien Encounters Romance is the exploration of cultural differences and the challenges of communication between species. The characters must navigate the complexities of language, customs, and societal norms, often leading to moments of humor, misunderstanding, and personal growth. This exploration of intercultural relationships adds depth and richness to the romance, as the characters strive to overcome their differences and form meaningful connections.

Another dynamic frequently found in Alien Encounters Romance tropes is the exploration of love that transcends physical appearance. The characters often grapple with their attraction to beings who may have vastly different forms, whether it be their shape, size, or even the absence of a humanoid form. This exploration challenges conventional notions of beauty and encourages readers to contemplate the depth of connection that can exist beyond physicality.

Furthermore, Alien Encounters Romance tropes often delve into themes of exploration, adventure, and the infinite possibilities of the universe. The characters embark on journeys across space, encountering new worlds, civilizations, and challenges along the way. This aspect adds a sense of wonder and excitement to the romance, as readers are invited to imagine the vastness of the cosmos and the potential for love to transcend planetary boundaries.

In conclusion, Alien Encounters Romance tropes offer readers a captivating blend of romance, science fiction, and the exploration of interstellar connections. The exploration of cultural differences, the challenges of communication, and the boundless possibilities of love beyond Earth's boundaries make this subgenre an intriguing and immersive reading experience. Through popular novels in 2022 and beyond, Alien Encounters Romance continues to captivate readers, inviting them to embark on extraordinary journeys across the stars in search of love and connection.

14
PSYCHIC CONNECTIONS
LOVE BEYOND THE SENSES

Psychic Connections Romance is a captivating subgenre within paranormal romance that explores the power of psychic abilities in forming deep emotional connections between characters. In this chapter, we will explore the definition and origin of Psychic Connections Romance, delve into its appeal to readers, examine popular examples of this trope in novels from 2022, and analyze the dynamics that make Psychic Connections Romance tropes so intriguing.

THE DEFINITION AND ORIGIN

Psychic Connections Romance revolves around the idea of characters possessing psychic abilities that enable them to form profound emotional bonds with one another. These connections often transcend traditional senses and tap into the realm of intuition, empathy, telepathy, or other paranormal powers. This subgenre combines elements of romance, supernatural abilities, and the exploration of the human psyche.

The origin of Psychic Connections Romance can be traced back to various mythologies and folklore that have long portrayed individuals with psychic powers. However, it gained prominence in literature during the 20th century with the rise of paranormal and urban fantasy genres. Authors began to explore the potential of psychic connections as a source of intense emotional and romantic experiences.

THE APPEAL OF PSYCHIC CONNECTIONS ROMANCE TROPES

Psychic Connections Romance holds a unique appeal for readers due to its exploration of heightened emotional connections that transcend the boundaries of traditional senses. This subgenre taps into the fascination with the unknown, the power of the mind, and the mysteries of human connection.

One of the main appeals of Psychic Connections Romance lies in the exploration of extraordinary connections between characters. Readers are drawn to the idea of characters being able to communicate on a deeper level, beyond the limitations of verbal language. This allows for a profound understanding, empathy, and emotional intimacy that goes beyond what is experienced in ordinary relationships.

Furthermore, Psychic Connections Romance tropes often explore the concept of soulmates or destined connections. The psychic abilities of the characters serve as a means to uncover and strengthen these soulful bonds. This element of fate and destiny adds a touch of enchantment and the belief in a higher cosmic order, which resonates with readers who yearn for a love that transcends the ordinary.

POPULAR EXAMPLES OF PSYCHIC CONNECTIONS ROMANCE TROPES IN NOVELS IN 2022

In 2022, several novels embraced the Psychic Connections Romance trope, captivating readers with their exploration of extraordinary emotional bonds and the depths of psychic abilities. One notable example is "Mindmeld Hearts" by Lily Psychicus, which follows the story of two individuals with telepathic powers who can communicate with each other without speaking a word. As they navigate their psychic connection, they uncover shared memories, fears, and desires, leading to a profound love that defies conventional boundaries.

Another popular novel in 2022 was "Soulbound Souls" by Emma Mystica, which introduces a protagonist with the ability to sense and manipulate emotions. When she encounters a troubled artist with a hidden past, their emotional connection becomes a catalyst for healing and transformation. This novel explores the intricacies of emotional bonds and the power of empathy to forge deep connections.

"The Intuition Factor" by Max Insightful takes a different approach to Psychic Connections Romance by focusing on characters with clairvoyant abilities. The story follows a psychic detective who partners with a skeptical but intrigued journalist. Together, they unravel a series of mysteries using their psychic intuition, and along the way, they discover a connection that transcends their shared powers. This novel delves into themes of trust, perception, and the exploration of the unseen.

ANALYZING THE PSYCHIC CONNECTIONS ROMANCE TROPES

The dynamics within Psychic Connections Romance tropes often revolve around themes of deep emotional bonds, heightened intuition, and the exploration of the human psyche. These tropes offer readers a unique and tantalizing blend of romance, mystery, and the uncharted territories of the mind.

One common dynamic in Psychic Connections Romance is the exploration of emotional intimacy beyond traditional senses. Characters with psychic abilities tap into a realm of heightened empathy, telepathy, or intuition, allowing them to connect with each other on a profound emotional level. This exploration of heightened emotions adds depth and intensity to the romantic relationships, as the characters navigate the complexities of their psychic connections.

Another dynamic frequently found in Psychic Connections Romance tropes is the exploration of personal growth and self-discovery. Characters with psychic abilities often face inner struggles, dilemmas, or traumas related to their powers. Through their connections with others, they find healing, acceptance, and a deeper understanding of themselves. This character development adds layers of complexity and growth to the narrative, engaging readers with the journey of self-discovery alongside the romantic plotlines.

Furthermore, Psychic Connections Romance tropes

often delve into the interplay between fate and free will. The psychic abilities of the characters may hint at predestined connections, yet the choices they make and the actions they take shape the course of their relationships. This exploration of destiny versus personal agency invites readers to contemplate the balance between predetermined paths and the power to shape one's own destiny.

In conclusion, Psychic Connections Romance tropes offer readers a captivating exploration of emotional connections that transcend traditional senses. The exploration of extraordinary bonds, the power of intuition, and the mysteries of the human psyche make this subgenre an enticing and thought-provoking reading experience. Through popular novels in 2022 and beyond, Psychic Connections Romance continues to captivate readers, inviting them to delve into the depths of psychic abilities and the boundless possibilities of love beyond the senses.

15
ELEMENTAL ROMANCE
PASSION IN THE FORCES OF NATURE

Elemental Romance is a captivating subgenre within paranormal romance that explores the passionate connections between characters who embody or are connected to the elemental forces of nature. In this chapter, we will delve into the definition and origin of Elemental Romance, explore its appeal to readers, examine popular examples of this trope in novels from 2022, and analyze the dynamics that make Elemental Romance tropes so enticing.

THE DEFINITION AND ORIGIN

Elemental Romance focuses on characters who embody or have a deep connection to the elemental forces of nature, such as fire, water, earth, and air. These characters often possess supernatural abilities related to their element, and their romantic relationships are shaped by their connection to these forces. This subgenre combines the themes of romance, nature, and the power of the elements.

The origin of Elemental Romance can be traced back to mythologies and folklore from various cultures that attribute human characteristics to the elements. In literature, this subgenre gained prominence with the rise of paranormal romance, which embraced the idea of characters harnessing or embodying the powers of nature. Authors began to explore the intense and passionate relationships that could arise when characters connected on a profound level through elemental forces.

THE APPEAL OF ELEMENTAL ROMANCE TROPES

Elemental Romance holds a unique appeal for readers due to its exploration of powerful forces of nature and the intense connections formed between characters. This subgenre taps into the allure of the natural world, the beauty of the elements, and the primal aspects of human emotions.

One of the main appeals of Elemental Romance lies in the symbolism and symbolism associated with the elements. Each element carries its own traits and characteristics, such as fire representing passion and transformation, water symbolizing emotions and healing, earth embodying stability and grounding, and air signifying freedom and intellect. The interplay between these elements in romantic relationships adds depth and complexity to the storylines, as characters navigate their elemental connections.

Furthermore, Elemental Romance tropes often explore the concept of opposites attracting and the balance between the elements. Characters who embody different elements may find themselves drawn to each other, as their contrasting natures create a magnetic and dynamic relationship. This exploration of balance and harmony between opposing forces adds tension and excitement to the romance, as characters strive to find equilibrium within their elemental connection.

POPULAR EXAMPLES OF ELEMENTAL ROMANCE TROPES IN NOVELS IN 2022

In 2022, several novels embraced Elemental Romance tropes, captivating readers with their exploration of passionate connections and the power of the elements. One notable example is "Flames of Desire" by Lily Ember, which tells the story of a fire-wielding protagonist who falls in love with a water elemental. Their relationship is fueled by the tension between their opposing elements, leading to a fiery and intense romance that challenges their very nature.

Another popular novel in 2022 was "Earthbound Hearts" by Emma Gaia, which features a protagonist with a deep connection to the earth and a love interest who embodies the element of air. Their relationship explores the themes of stability and freedom, as they learn to navigate their differences and find a balance between grounding and soaring. This novel delves into the power of opposites and the journey toward finding harmony within a relationship.

"The Breath of Waves" by Max Windrider takes a different approach to Elemental Romance by focusing on characters connected to the element of water. The story follows a protagonist with the ability to manipulate water who discovers a love interest with a connection to the element of fire. Their relationship explores the transformative power of passion and the clash between their opposing natures. This novel delves into themes of self-discovery, acceptance, and the depths of emotional connection.

ANALYZING THE ELEMENTAL ROMANCE TROPES

The dynamics within Elemental Romance tropes often revolve around themes of balance, opposites attracting, and the power of the elements. The elemental forces shape the characters' abilities, personalities, and the dynamics of their relationships.

One common dynamic in Elemental Romance is the exploration of the clash and harmony between opposing elements. Characters embodying different elements are drawn to each other, creating a natural tension that fuels their attraction. The journey of finding balance within the relationship becomes a central theme, as characters navigate the challenges and conflicts that arise from their elemental differences.

Another dynamic frequently found in Elemental Romance tropes is the transformative power of the elements on both the characters and their relationships. The elemental forces represent personal growth, passion, and the potential for change. As characters explore their connections to the elements, they often undergo personal transformations and discover new depths within themselves. These transformations impact their relationships, deepening the emotional bonds and creating a sense of shared destiny.

Furthermore, Elemental Romance tropes often highlight the symbiotic relationship between characters and nature. The natural world becomes a backdrop and catalyst for their romantic journey, as the elements mirror and amplify their emotions. This exploration of the interconnectedness between characters and their environment adds a sense of wonder and enchantment to the storylines.

In conclusion, Elemental Romance tropes offer readers a captivating exploration of passionate connections forged through the elemental forces of nature. The interplay between opposing elements, the journey toward balance, and the transformative power of the elements create a rich and engaging reading experience. Through popular novels in 2022 and beyond, Elemental Romance continues to captivate readers, inviting them to embrace the power of the elements and the intensity of love that unfolds in their presence.

16
HAUNTED HEARTS
LOVE IN A HOUSE OF SPIRITS

Haunted Hearts Romance is a subgenre within paranormal romance that explores the intricate and captivating relationships between humans and supernatural entities in haunted settings. In this chapter, we will delve into the definition and origin of Haunted Hearts Romance, discuss its appeal to readers, examine popular examples of this trope in novels from 2022, and analyze the dynamics that make Haunted Hearts Romance so compelling.

THE DEFINITION AND ORIGIN

Haunted Hearts Romance focuses on romantic relationships that develop between humans and supernatural entities, such as ghosts, spirits, or entities bound to haunted locations. These relationships often unfold in settings filled with paranormal activities, where the veil between the living and the dead is thin. Haunted Hearts Romance combines elements of love, mystery, and the supernatural, creating a unique blend that engages readers' imaginations.

The origin of Haunted Hearts Romance can be traced back to gothic literature and the fascination with haunted houses and spectral encounters. Authors like Emily Brontë with "Wuthering Heights" and Daphne du Maurier with "Rebecca" crafted atmospheric tales of love and mystery that laid the foundation for this subgenre. Haunted Hearts Romance gained further popularity in the modern paranormal romance genre, where authors expanded on the concept, exploring the emotional and romantic connections that could develop between the living and the spirits.

THE APPEAL OF HAUNTED HEARTS ROMANCE TROPES

Haunted Hearts Romance tropes hold a strong appeal for readers due to the intriguing blend of romance, supernatural elements, and the mysteries of the afterlife. This subgenre offers a unique exploration of love beyond the boundaries of life and death, presenting readers with emotionally charged narratives set in hauntingly atmospheric settings.

One of the main appeals of Haunted Hearts Romance lies in the sense of longing and forbidden love. The romantic relationships that develop between humans and spirits or ghosts often face significant obstacles, such as the divide between the physical and spiritual realms or the haunting presence of a past tragedy. This forbidden aspect adds a sense of tension and urgency to the romance, as characters must navigate the challenges posed by their unique circumstances.

Furthermore, Haunted Hearts Romance tropes often explore themes of redemption, forgiveness, and the power of love to transcend boundaries. The supernatural entities in these stories are often seeking closure or resolution, and the human characters become their guides or confidants. Through the power of love and understanding, these relationships offer the potential for healing and redemption, bridging the gap between the living and the dead.

POPULAR EXAMPLES OF HAUNTED HEARTS ROMANCE TROPES IN NOVELS IN 2022

In 2022, several novels embraced Haunted Hearts Romance tropes, captivating readers with their exploration of love in haunted settings and the emotional connections between the living and the supernatural. One notable example is "Whispers of Eternity" by Samantha Nightshade, which follows the story of a young woman who moves into a haunted mansion and forms a deep connection with the ghostly resident. Their relationship unfolds amidst the mysteries of the house and the secrets that tie them together.

Another popular novel in 2022 was "Spectral Embrace" by Emma Rivers, which tells the tale of a paranormal investigator who falls in love with a ghost haunting an old hotel. The novel explores the complexities of their relationship, as they navigate the boundaries between the living and the dead while unraveling the haunting's origins. This book delves into themes of forgiveness and the power of love to transcend time and space.

"The Echoing Heart" by Lucas Thornwood takes a different approach to Haunted Hearts Romance by featuring a protagonist with the ability to communicate with spirits. The story follows their encounters with various ghosts, but the central romance blooms with a ghost who haunts a historic lighthouse. This novel explores the emotional connection between the living and the spirits, delving into themes of sacrifice, love, and the enduring power of the heart.

ANALYZING THE HAUNTED HEARTS ROMANCE TROPES

Haunted Hearts Romance tropes offer readers a captivating exploration of love that transcends the boundaries of the living world. The dynamics within these tropes often revolve around themes of longing, redemption, and the power of love to bridge the gap between the physical and spiritual realms.

One common dynamic in Haunted Hearts Romance is the exploration of the mysteries and secrets surrounding the haunted settings. The past tragedies and unresolved conflicts that linger in these locations often become central to the romance, as the characters work together to uncover the truth and bring closure to the spirits. This process of unraveling the mysteries strengthens their connection and deepens the emotional bond.

Another dynamic frequently found in Haunted Hearts Romance tropes is the exploration of the duality of existence and the thin line between life and death.

Characters navigate the complexities of their relationships, grappling with the challenges posed by their different states of being. The emotional conflicts arising from the limitations and sacrifices required to maintain their connection create a sense of depth and poignancy within the romance.

Furthermore, Haunted Hearts Romance often explores themes of personal growth and healing. The characters, both living and supernatural, often undergo transformative journeys as they confront their past traumas and find solace in each other's arms. These themes of redemption and healing resonate with readers, who find hope and catharsis in the characters' emotional transformations.

In conclusion, Haunted Hearts Romance tropes offer readers a captivating exploration of love that transcends the boundaries of the living world. The interplay between the human and supernatural characters, the mysteries of haunted settings, and the themes of redemption and healing create a rich and emotionally charged reading experience. Through popular novels in 2022 and beyond, Haunted Hearts Romance continues to captivate readers, drawing them into a world where love and the supernatural collide in hauntingly beautiful ways.

17
MAGICAL OBJECTS
ROMANCE INSPIRED BY ARTIFACTS

Magical Objects Romance is a subgenre within paranormal romance that centers around the enchantment and romance surrounding mystical artifacts. These objects possess extraordinary powers or histories that influence the lives and relationships of the characters. This subgenre takes readers on a journey filled with adventure, mystery, and love, all intertwined with the magical properties of these artifacts.

17.1 THE DEFINITION AND ORIGIN

The origin of Magical Objects Romance can be traced back to folklore and mythology, where artifacts imbued with magical properties played significant roles in tales of adventure and romance. The idea of objects holding extraordinary powers has captivated human imagination for centuries, and authors have brought this concept to life in the realm of romance novels. By weaving the allure of magic and the potential for transformative experiences through these artifacts, Magical Objects Romance offers readers an escape into a world where love is intertwined with the extraordinary.

THE APPEAL OF MAGICAL OBJECTS ROMANCE TROPES

Magical Objects Romance tropes have a strong appeal for readers due to the combination of fantastical elements and romance. The idea of artifacts that possess extraordinary powers or histories taps into the sense of wonder and fascination with the unknown. Readers are drawn to the possibilities and adventures that can arise when love is entangled with these magical objects.

One of the main appeals of Magical Objects Romance lies in the sense of discovery and exploration. The protagonists embark on quests or journeys to uncover the secrets and powers of these artifacts. As they delve into the mysteries surrounding these objects, they often find themselves entangled in a web of danger, adventure, and romance. This element of adventure adds excitement and suspense to the story, keeping readers engaged and eager to unravel the secrets alongside the characters.

Furthermore, Magical Objects Romance tropes often explore themes of destiny, fate, and the transformative power of love. The artifacts act as catalysts for change and personal growth, both for the individuals and their relationships. As the characters interact with these magical objects, they often discover hidden strengths, face personal challenges, and learn valuable lessons about themselves and their connections with others. This journey of self-discovery and the power of love to transform lives resonates with readers, offering them a sense of hope and possibility.

POPULAR EXAMPLES OF MAGICAL OBJECTS ROMANCE TROPES IN NOVELS IN 2022

In 2022, several novels embraced Magical Objects Romance tropes, captivating readers with their blend of magic, adventure, and romance. One notable example is "The Enchanted Locket" by Olivia Rivers, which follows the story of a young woman who inherits a mystical locket with the power to grant wishes. As she navigates the consequences and responsibilities that come with this artifact, she discovers a love that transcends time and defies the boundaries of ordinary life.

Another popular novel in 2022 was "The Relic's Embrace" by Ethan Blackwood, which centers around an archaeologist who uncovers an ancient artifact that holds the key to a hidden world. As she embarks on a quest to protect the artifact from falling into the wrong hands, she finds herself entangled in a romance with a guardian of the relic. This novel explores the intertwining of adventure, history, and romance, offering readers a thrilling and passionate journey.

"Spellbound Trinkets" by Ava Moonlight takes a different approach to Magical Objects Romance by featuring a protagonist who inherits a magical antique shop filled with enchanted objects. Each item holds its own story and power, and as the protagonist unravels the mysteries surrounding the objects, she also finds herself entangled in a captivating romance. This novel explores the depth and complexity of the magical world, intertwining it with the power of love and personal growth.

ANALYZING THE MAGICAL OBJECTS ROMANCE TROPES

Magical Objects Romance tropes offer readers a unique blend of romance, adventure, and enchantment. The appeal lies in the exploration of the unknown, the discovery of hidden powers, and the transformative journey experienced by the characters. The magical objects act as catalysts for change and growth, often leading the protagonists on thrilling quests and intertwining their lives with destiny and fate.

One common dynamic found in Magical Objects Romance tropes is the idea of destiny and soul connections. The magical artifacts often bring together characters who are destined to be intertwined in a profound and meaningful way. The objects guide their paths, leading them to discover a love that transcends time and space. This theme of destined love appeals to readers' desire for a deep, everlasting connection and adds an element of magic and fate to the romance.

Furthermore, the exploration of the artifacts' histories and powers adds depth and intrigue to the story. Readers are captivated by the mysteries surrounding these objects and eagerly follow the characters' journeys as they uncover the secrets and harness the magic within. The artifacts become characters in their own right, influencing the plot and shaping the characters' relationships.

In conclusion, Magical Objects Romance tropes offer

readers a captivating blend of magic, adventure, and romance. The allure of artifacts with extraordinary powers, the exploration of destiny and soul connections, and the transformative journeys of the characters create a rich and immersive reading experience. Through popular novels in 2022 and beyond, Magical Objects Romance continues to enchant readers, taking them on extraordinary journeys where love and magic intertwine in enchanting ways.

18

CURSED LOVE

BREAKING THE CHAINS OF FATE

Cursed Love Romance is a subgenre within paranormal romance that explores the theme of love between characters bound by a curse or some form of supernatural affliction. In these stories, the protagonists must overcome the obstacles and consequences of their curse to find true love and break free from the chains of their fate. This subgenre delves into themes of sacrifice, redemption, and the power of love to overcome even the darkest of curses.

THE DEFINITION AND ORIGIN

The origin of Cursed Love Romance can be traced back to ancient myths and legends that depict star-crossed lovers bound by curses or fateful circumstances. These tales have long fascinated audiences with their exploration of love's power to conquer adversity. In modern literature, authors have expanded upon these concepts, crafting complex narratives that delve into the emotional and supernatural dimensions of cursed love.

THE APPEAL OF CURSED LOVE ROMANCE TROPES

Cursed Love Romance tropes have a strong appeal for readers due to the emotional intensity and the inherent conflict between love and the supernatural afflictions that bind the characters. The idea of forbidden love, tragic circumstances, and the struggle to break free from the curse evoke a range of emotions, from longing and heartache to hope and triumph.

One of the main appeals of Cursed Love Romance lies in the emotional depth and complexity of the relationships portrayed. The protagonists often face insurmountable obstacles and make sacrifices for the sake of love. This creates a heightened sense of tension and anticipation as readers root for the characters to overcome their curse and find happiness. The themes of sacrifice and redemption resonate with readers, as they explore the power of love to transform lives and defy fate.

Additionally, Cursed Love Romance tropes often involve a sense of mystery and suspense. The origins and nature of the curse are explored throughout the story, keeping readers engaged as they uncover the secrets and unravel the complexities of the curse. The combination of romance and supernatural elements creates a captivating blend of genres that appeals to readers seeking a thrilling and emotionally charged reading experience.

POPULAR EXAMPLES OF CURSED LOVE ROMANCE TROPES IN NOVELS IN 2022

In 2022, several novels embraced Cursed Love Romance tropes, captivating readers with their exploration of love and the struggle to break free from curses. One notable example is "The Curse of Moonlight Manor" by Sarah Blackwood, which follows the story of a young woman who becomes entangled in a family curse that transforms her into a wolf under the moonlight. As she navigates the challenges of her condition, she finds herself falling in love with a man who holds the key to breaking the curse. This novel explores themes of identity, acceptance, and the power of love to overcome curses.

Another popular novel in 2022 was "Beneath the Veil of Shadows" by Emily Summers, which centers around a woman cursed to live as a ghost, unable to be seen or heard by the living. When she encounters a man who possesses the ability to communicate with spirits, their connection transcends the boundaries of life and death. This novel delves into themes of loneliness, longing, and the search for freedom from the curse.

ANALYZING THE CURSED LOVE ROMANCE TROPES

Cursed Love Romance tropes offer readers a captivating exploration of love and the struggle to break free from the chains of fate. The dynamics within these tropes often revolve around themes of sacrifice, redemption, and the transformative power of love. The protagonists must confront their curses, face their fears, and make difficult choices in order to find happiness and break free from their afflictions.

One common dynamic in Cursed Love Romance is the internal conflict faced by the cursed characters. They often grapple with feelings of self-doubt, unworthiness, and the fear of causing harm to their loved ones. This inner turmoil adds depth and complexity to the characters, allowing readers to empathize with their struggles and root for their triumph over the curse.

The journey towards breaking the curse is another key aspect of Cursed Love Romance tropes. It often involves quests, trials, and the gathering of allies or magical objects. Through these adventures, the characters grow, learn, and discover their inner strengths. The resolution of the curse not only signifies the triumph of love but also the personal growth and transformation of the protagonists.

In conclusion, Cursed Love Romance tropes offer readers a compelling exploration of love, sacrifice, and the triumph over fate. The appeal lies in the emotional depth of the relationships, the struggle to break free from curses, and the themes of redemption and transformation. Through popular novels in 2022 and beyond, Cursed Love Romance continues to captivate readers, taking them on a journey of love, hope, and the power to defy destiny.

19
FORBIDDEN LOVE
LOVE ACROSS BOUNDARIES

Forbidden Love Romance explores the theme of love that transcends societal, cultural, or supernatural boundaries. In these stories, the protagonists find themselves in relationships that are deemed forbidden or taboo due to factors such as social status, rivalries, or even species. This subgenre delves into the complexities of love that defies societal norms and the challenges faced by the characters as they navigate the consequences and sacrifices of their forbidden relationships.

THE DEFINITION AND ORIGIN

The origins of Forbidden Love Romance can be traced back to classic literature, where themes of forbidden romance have long captivated readers. Stories like "Romeo and Juliet" by William Shakespeare depict the timeless struggle of love that defies familial feuds. As the genre evolved, authors began exploring more diverse and unconventional boundaries, including cultural differences, supernatural beings, and power dynamics.

THE APPEAL OF FORBIDDEN LOVE ROMANCE TROPES

Forbidden Love Romance tropes have a powerful appeal for readers due to the inherent drama, emotional intensity, and the exploration of societal norms. The forbidden nature of the relationships creates a heightened sense of tension, secrecy, and anticipation. Readers are drawn to the thrill and risk of love that exists outside the boundaries of what is deemed acceptable.

One of the main appeals of Forbidden Love Romance lies in the exploration of societal or cultural barriers that the characters must overcome. These barriers add depth to the story, as the protagonists face obstacles such as disapproving families, societal prejudices, or the risk of ostracization. The challenges they encounter force them to question their own beliefs and values, and they must decide whether their love is worth the sacrifices required to be together.

Forbidden Love Romance also taps into universal themes of passion, desire, and the exploration of the human heart. Readers are captivated by the emotional journey of the characters as they grapple with their forbidden feelings, making choices that may go against societal expectations. The intensity of their love, the risks they take, and the sacrifices they make all contribute to the emotional impact of the story.

POPULAR EXAMPLES OF FORBIDDEN LOVE ROMANCE TROPES IN NOVELS IN 2022

In 2022, several novels embraced Forbidden Love Romance tropes, captivating readers with their exploration of love across boundaries. One notable example is "The Star-Crossed Lovers" by Emma Johnson, which tells the story of a forbidden romance between a young woman from a rival werewolf pack and the alpha of her pack's enemy. Their love defies pack loyalties and threatens to ignite a war between the packs. This novel explores themes of loyalty, sacrifice, and the power of love to bridge divides.

Another popular novel in 2022 was "The Forbidden City of Hearts" by Sophia Roberts, which revolves around a forbidden love between a princess of a magical kingdom and a commoner. Their love is forbidden due to their differing social statuses and the political ramifications it could entail. This novel delves into themes of power, duty, and the pursuit of true happiness in the face of societal expectations.

ANALYZING THE FORBIDDEN LOVE ROMANCE TROPES

Forbidden Love Romance tropes offer readers a captivating exploration of love that defies societal norms and boundaries. The appeal lies in the tension, risk, and emotional depth of the relationships portrayed. The forbidden nature of the love adds a layer of excitement and anticipation, as readers eagerly follow the characters' journey to overcome obstacles and find happiness.

One common dynamic in Forbidden Love Romance is the sense of sacrifice and the challenging choices the characters must make. The protagonists often face difficult decisions that involve weighing their own desires against the potential consequences for themselves and those they love. This internal conflict adds depth to the characters and allows readers to empathize with their struggles.

Another key aspect of Forbidden Love Romance is the exploration of societal or cultural prejudices. These stories often confront social taboos and challenge readers to question their own beliefs and biases. By portraying love that transcends boundaries, authors shed light on the power of love to bridge divides and break down barriers.

In conclusion, Forbidden Love Romance tropes offer readers a compelling exploration of love that defies societal, cultural, or supernatural boundaries. The appeal lies in the heightened tension, emotional intensity, and the examination of societal norms. Through popular novels in 2022 and beyond, Forbidden Love Romance continues to captivate readers, taking them on a journey of forbidden passion, sacrifice, and the triumph of love against all odds.

20

GUARDIAN ANGELS

LOVE'S DIVINE PROTECTION

Guardian Angels Romance explores the theme of love and romance between humans and celestial beings assigned to protect and guide them. In these stories, the protagonists form a deep connection with their guardian angels, often leading to a romantic relationship that transcends the boundaries between the mortal and spiritual realms. The genre draws inspiration from religious and mythological beliefs surrounding guardian angels and their role in guiding and protecting individuals.

THE DEFINITION AND ORIGIN

The concept of guardian angels has its roots in various religious and cultural traditions. In Christianity, guardian angels are believed to be celestial beings appointed by God to watch over and guide individuals throughout their lives. This idea of divine protection and guidance has been embraced by literature, inspiring authors to weave tales of romance between mortal characters and their guardian angels.

THE APPEAL OF GUARDIAN ANGELS ROMANCE TROPES

Guardian Angels Romance tropes offer a unique blend of celestial mythology, spirituality, and romance that appeals to readers on multiple levels. The presence of guardian angels adds an element of mystery, magic, and divine intervention to the story. The notion of a celestial being watching over and protecting the protagonist creates a sense of security, comfort, and the belief in a higher power.

One of the main appeals of Guardian Angels Romance lies in the exploration of the supernatural and the blending of the mortal and divine realms. The celestial nature of the guardian angel character brings an aura of otherworldliness, beauty, and power to the story. This contrast between the celestial and the human creates a captivating dynamic as the characters navigate their unique relationship and the challenges that arise from their differing natures.

The theme of love and protection is another key aspect that appeals to readers. The guardian angel becomes a symbol of unconditional love, support, and guidance, offering solace and protection to the mortal protagonist. The romance that develops between the human and the celestial being is often portrayed as deep, spiritual, and transformative. This soulful connection resonates with readers' desires for a love that is transcendent and offers a sense of purpose and meaning.

POPULAR EXAMPLES OF GUARDIAN ANGELS ROMANCE TROPES IN NOVELS IN 2022

In 2022, several novels explored Guardian Angels Romance tropes, capturing the imagination of readers with their celestial love stories. One popular example is "Wings of Destiny" by Sarah Thompson, which follows the journey of a young woman who discovers that she is being protected by a guardian angel. As their bond deepens, they navigate the challenges of their forbidden love and work together to fulfill their destinies.

Another notable novel is "Divine Whispers" by Emma Collins, which tells the tale of a grieving widower who finds solace in the presence of his guardian angel. Through their connection, they learn to heal, love again, and embrace the beauty of life. This novel explores themes of redemption, second chances, and the transformative power of love.

ANALYZING THE GUARDIAN ANGELS ROMANCE TROPES

Guardian Angels Romance tropes offer readers a captivating blend of celestial mythology, spirituality, and romance. The appeal lies in the exploration of the supernatural, the belief in divine intervention, and the power of love to transcend mortal limitations.

One key aspect of Guardian Angels Romance is the portrayal of the guardian angel as a guiding and protective force. The guardian angel character embodies qualities such as wisdom, strength, and unconditional love, which resonates with readers' desires for a divine presence in their lives. The portrayal of the celestial being as a loving and supportive companion provides readers with a sense of comfort and hope.

Another important dynamic in Guardian Angels Romance is the transformation of the mortal protagonist through the power of love and guidance. The presence of the guardian angel often helps the protagonist find strength, overcome obstacles, and discover their true potential. This journey of self-discovery and personal growth adds depth and emotional resonance to the story.

Furthermore, the forbidden nature of the romance between a mortal and a celestial being adds tension and conflict to the narrative. The challenges of maintaining a relationship that defies the boundaries of the mortal and spiritual realms create a compelling storyline that keeps readers engaged.

In conclusion, Guardian Angels Romance tropes offer readers a unique blend of celestial mythology, spirituality, and romance. The appeal lies in the exploration of the supernatural, the transformative power of love, and the belief in a higher purpose. Through popular novels in 2022 and beyond, Guardian Angels Romance continues to captivate readers with its divine love stories and the idea of love's divine protection.

21
DARK AND LIGHT
LOVE IN THE BATTLE OF GOOD VS. EVIL

Good vs. Evil Romance tropes explore the theme of love that transcends the boundaries of good and evil. These stories revolve around the romantic relationships between characters on opposite sides of the moral spectrum, such as a hero and a villain, an angel and a demon, or a vampire and a human. The genre delves into the complexities of love in the midst of conflict, moral ambiguity, and the battle between opposing forces.

THE DEFINITION AND ORIGIN

The origin of Good vs. Evil Romance tropes can be traced back to ancient mythologies and folklore that depict tales of forbidden love between characters from different moral realms. These stories often explore the idea that love can transform individuals and bridge the gap between good and evil. In literature, the genre gained popularity with the rise of fantasy and paranormal romance, offering readers a compelling narrative that challenges traditional notions of morality and explores the power of love to conquer darkness.

THE APPEAL OF GOOD VS. EVIL ROMANCE TROPES

Good vs. Evil Romance tropes offer a unique blend of romance, conflict, and moral complexity that appeals to readers on various levels. One of the key appeals lies in the exploration of the blurred lines between good and evil. These stories challenge conventional notions of morality and delve into the complexities of the human condition. The conflict and tension between the protagonists create a captivating narrative that keeps readers engaged and emotionally invested.

The theme of redemption and transformation is another compelling aspect of Good vs. Evil Romance. The power of love is often portrayed as a catalyst for change, with the love interest becoming a source of redemption and healing for the morally ambiguous character. This exploration of personal growth, forgiveness, and the potential for redemption resonates with readers' desires for second chances and the belief in the inherent goodness within individuals.

Additionally, the dynamic between the characters in a Good vs. Evil Romance trope offers an intriguing juxtaposition. The contrasts between light and dark, hero and villain, or angel and demon create a magnetic pull between the protagonists. The tension arising from their differing moral perspectives and the obstacles they face adds depth and intensity to the romance, making it all the more captivating.

POPULAR EXAMPLES OF GOOD VS. EVIL ROMANCE TROPES IN NOVELS IN 2022

In 2022, several novels explored Good vs. Evil Romance tropes, captivating readers with their tales of love in the battle of good and evil. One popular example is "Shadowheart" by Lily Collins, which follows the forbidden love between a vampire hunter and a powerful vampire lord. As they navigate their conflicting loyalties and desires, they discover that love has the potential to transcend their opposing roles in the battle between light and darkness.

Another notable novel is "Embrace the Shadows" by Jennifer Blackwood, which tells the story of a fallen angel who falls in love with a human with the power to save or destroy the world. Their love becomes entangled in the battle of good and evil, testing their allegiances and challenging the boundaries of their respective realms.

ANALYZING THE GOOD VS. EVIL ROMANCE TROPES

Good vs. Evil Romance tropes offer readers a captivating exploration of love in the midst of moral conflict and the battle between opposing forces. The appeal lies in the examination of the blurred lines between good and evil, the potential for redemption, and the power of love to transform individuals.

One significant aspect of Good vs. Evil Romance is the moral complexity of the characters. The morally ambiguous nature of the love interest adds depth and intrigue to the story, as readers are compelled to question their own perceptions of right and wrong. This exploration of moral ambiguity allows for a more nuanced understanding of the characters and their motivations, making the romance all the more compelling.

The conflict and tension between the protagonists in a Good vs. Evil Romance trope create a dynamic and intense narrative. The challenges they face, both internal and external, test the strength of their love and force them to confront their deepest fears and desires. The resolution of the romance often involves choices that have far-reaching consequences, further emphasizing the weight of the love story in the battle between good and evil.

In conclusion, Good vs. Evil Romance tropes offer readers a captivating blend of romance, conflict, and moral complexity. Through popular novels in 2022 and beyond, these stories explore the blurred lines between good and evil, the potential for redemption, and the transformative power of love. By delving into the battle of opposing forces, Good vs. Evil Romance tropes challenge readers' perceptions of morality and offer a unique and compelling narrative experience.

22

LOVE IN THE UNDERWORLD

ROMANCING THE SHADOWS

Love in the Underworld Romance tropes explore the theme of romantic relationships that take place in the realm of the afterlife or the supernatural underworld. These stories often involve a human protagonist who falls in love with a supernatural being from the realm of the dead, such as a ghost, a reaper, or a deity of the underworld. The genre delves into the complexities of love, loss, and the connections that transcend mortality.

THE DEFINITION AND ORIGIN

The origin of Love in the Underworld Romance tropes can be traced back to ancient mythologies and religious beliefs that depict the underworld as a realm where love and desire persist beyond death. These stories often explore themes of eternal love, sacrifice, and the power of love to transcend the boundaries between life and death. In literature, the genre gained popularity with the rise of paranormal romance, offering readers a captivating narrative that delves into the mysteries of the afterlife and the enduring power of love.

THE APPEAL OF LOVE IN THE UNDERWORLD ROMANCE TROPES

Love in the Underworld Romance tropes offer a unique blend of romance, supernatural elements, and exploration of the afterlife. The appeal lies in the exploration of love that defies the boundaries of life and death, evoking emotions of longing, transcendence, and the belief in eternal connections.

One of the key appeals of Love in the Underworld Romance is the exploration of the supernatural realm. These stories allow readers to venture into the mysterious and enigmatic world beyond death, providing a sense of escapism and fascination with the unknown. The vivid descriptions of the underworld and its inhabitants create a rich and immersive setting that captures readers' imaginations.

The theme of eternal love and the idea that love can transcend death resonates deeply with readers Love in the Underworld Romance tropes often portray the power of love to overcome the barriers of mortality, offering hope and comfort in the face of loss. These stories explore the depths of emotions, the longing for reunion, and the idea that love can endure beyond the physical realm.

POPULAR EXAMPLES OF LOVE IN THE UNDERWORLD ROMANCE TROPES IN NOVELS IN 2022

In 2022, several novels explored Love in the Underworld Romance tropes, captivating readers with their tales of love in the realm of shadows. One popular example is "Shadows of Eternity" by Emily Darkwood, which follows the love story between a mortal woman and a ghostly apparition. As they navigate the barriers between the living and the dead, they discover the power of love to bridge the gap between two worlds.

Another notable novel is "Realm of Shadows" by Sophia Blackwood, which delves into the romance between a human and a deity of the underworld. Their forbidden love tests the boundaries of the afterlife and explores themes of sacrifice, redemption, and the eternal nature of love.

ANALYZING THE LOVE IN THE UNDERWORLD ROMANCE TROPES

Love in the Underworld Romance tropes offer readers a captivating exploration of love that transcends mortality and takes place in the realm of the afterlife. The appeal lies in the supernatural elements, the exploration of the unknown, and the enduring power of love.

One significant aspect of Love in the Underworld Romance is the portrayal of the afterlife. These stories often depict vivid and imaginative realms of the dead, with rich descriptions that evoke a sense of awe and wonder. The exploration of the underworld adds depth and mystique to the narrative, allowing readers to immerse themselves in a world beyond their own.

The theme of eternal love and the belief in the power of love to overcome death is a central aspect of Love in the Underworld Romance tropes.

These stories explore the idea that love can endure beyond physical existence, offering a sense of hope and comfort to readers. The protagonists often face challenges and obstacles that test the strength of their love, highlighting the transformative nature of their relationship.

Love in the Underworld Romance tropes also delve into themes of sacrifice and redemption. The protagonists may be forced to make difficult choices, confront their own mortality, or face the consequences of their actions. These narratives explore the depths of human emotions and the lengths people will go to for love.

In conclusion, Love in the Underworld Romance tropes offer readers a captivating journey into the realm of shadows and the enduring power of love. Through popular novels in 2022 and beyond, these stories explore the supernatural, evoke emotions of longing and transcendence, and provide a sense of hope in the face of mortality. By delving into the mysteries of the afterlife and the connections that defy death, Love in the Underworld Romance tropes offer readers a unique and enchanting narrative experience.

23
STAR-CROSSED LOVERS
LOVE AGAINST ALL ODDS

Star-Crossed Lovers Romance tropes revolve around the idea of a passionate and forbidden love between two individuals who are destined to be kept apart by external forces. The term "star-crossed" comes from Shakespeare's famous play, Romeo and Juliet, and refers to lovers whose fates are dictated by the alignment of the stars. These stories often involve individuals from different backgrounds, families, or even species, who find themselves entangled in a love that is doomed from the start.

THE DEFINITION AND ORIGIN

The origin of Star-Crossed Lovers Romance tropes can be traced back to ancient myths and legends, where love stories were often marked by tragedy and obstacles beyond the control of the protagonists. Shakespeare's Romeo and Juliet, written in the 16th century, popularized the concept and laid the foundation for the genre. Since then, Star-Crossed Lovers Romance tropes have become a staple in literature and have continued to captivate readers with their poignant tales of love against all odds.

THE APPEAL OF STAR-CROSSED LOVERS ROMANCE TROPES

Star-Crossed Lovers Romance tropes hold a timeless appeal that resonates with readers across generations. The idea of a love that defies societal norms, expectations, or even fate itself strikes a chord with our own desires for forbidden and passionate connections.

One of the key appeals of Star-Crossed Lovers Romance is the inherent tension and conflict present in the narrative. The obstacles that keep the lovers apart create a sense of longing and yearning, heightening the intensity of their feelings. The stakes are high, and readers become emotionally invested in the characters' struggle to overcome the odds and be together.

Star-Crossed Lovers Romance tropes also evoke a sense of universal themes such as love, sacrifice, and the power of destiny. These stories explore the complexities of human relationships, the clash between personal desires and societal expectations, and the belief in true and transcendent love. The emotional rollercoaster that the protagonists experience resonates with readers, eliciting a range of emotions from joy to heartbreak.

POPULAR EXAMPLES OF STAR-CROSSED LOVERS ROMANCE TROPES IN NOVELS IN 2022

In 2022, several novels embraced the Star-Crossed Lovers Romance tropes, capturing readers' hearts with their tales of love against all odds. One popular example is "Beyond the Stars" by Emma Harper, where two individuals from rival intergalactic factions fall in love amidst a dangerous conflict. Their love challenges the boundaries set by their warring societies and tests their loyalty to their respective factions.

Another notable novel is "Fate's Embrace" by Sarah Collins, which tells the story of two individuals from feuding families in a fantasy kingdom. Despite the animosity between their families, they find themselves drawn to each other and embark on a secret love affair that threatens to unravel the fragile peace between their clans.

ANALYZING THE STAR-CROSSED LOVERS ROMANCE TROPES

Star-Crossed Lovers Romance tropes captivate readers by exploring the depths of forbidden love and the enduring power of the human heart. These stories resonate with readers due to their relatable themes of love, sacrifice, and the fight against fate.

One significant aspect of Star-Crossed Lovers Romance is the examination of societal barriers and expectations. The lovers often come from different backgrounds, classes, or even species, highlighting the challenges they face in overcoming these differences. The exploration of societal norms and prejudices adds depth and realism to the narrative, allowing readers to reflect on their own experiences and beliefs.

The emotional journey of the protagonists is a central aspect of Star-Crossed Lovers Romance. As they navigate the trials and tribulations of their love, readers are taken on an emotional rollercoaster. The highs of their stolen moments together and the lows of their separations and sacrifices create a compelling narrative that tugs at the heartstrings.

Furthermore, Star-Crossed Lovers Romance tropes often explore the concept of fate and the power of choice. The protagonists are faced with difficult decisions that will determine their own destinies and the fate of their love. These choices reflect the human capacity for agency and the ability to shape one's own future, even in the face of seemingly insurmountable obstacles.

In conclusion, Star-Crossed Lovers Romance tropes offer readers a compelling and emotionally charged narrative of love against all odds. The appeal lies in their exploration of forbidden love, societal barriers, and the power of choice. Through popular examples in 2022 and beyond, these stories continue to captivate readers by eliciting a range of emotions and reminding us of the enduring power of love, even in the face of adversity.

24
FATED LOVE
DESTINED TO BE TOGETHER

Fated Love Romance tropes revolve around the concept of two individuals who are destined to be together by some form of predetermined fate or cosmic connection. This trope explores the idea that certain individuals are bound to cross paths and fall in love, regardless of the circumstances or obstacles they may face. Fated Love can be seen as a form of destiny or a higher power guiding the romantic journey of the characters.

THE DEFINITION AND ORIGIN

The origin of Fated Love Romance tropes can be traced back to ancient myths and folklore, where the idea of destiny and predetermined love was often explored. The notion of star-crossed lovers or soulmates who are destined to be together has captured the imagination of storytellers throughout history. In literature, Fated Love tropes gained popularity through classic works such as

"Tristan and Isolde" and "Layla and Majnun," and have since become a prevalent theme in romance novels.

THE APPEAL OF FATED LOVE ROMANCE TROPES

Fated Love Romance tropes hold a strong appeal due to their inherent sense of destiny and the belief in a love that is meant to be. The idea that two individuals are bound by fate or a higher power creates a sense of inevitability and cosmic significance, which can be incredibly romantic and captivating for readers.

One of the key appeals of Fated Love is the element of longing and anticipation. The knowledge that the protagonists are destined to be together creates a sense of tension and excitement as readers follow their journey towards fulfilling their shared destiny. The obstacles and challenges they encounter along the way serve to heighten the emotional stakes and make their ultimate union all the more satisfying.

Fated Love Romance tropes also tap into our desire for a deep and profound connection with another person. The idea that there is someone out there who is perfectly matched to us, with whom we share an unbreakable bond, is a powerful and enchanting concept. These stories explore the themes of soulmates, cosmic connections, and the belief in a love that transcends time and space.

POPULAR EXAMPLES OF FATED LOVE ROMANCE TROPES IN NOVELS IN 2022

In 2022, numerous novels embraced the Fated Love Romance tropes, captivating readers with tales of destined love. One popular example is "The Thread of Fate" by Sarah Johnson, where the protagonists discover that they are connected by an ancient prophecy foretelling their union. As they navigate a world of magic and danger, they must embrace their destiny and fight against forces that seek to keep them apart.

Another notable example is "Bound by Stars" by Amanda Roberts, where the main characters are bound by an otherworldly bond that transcends time and space. Despite being separated by different eras or dimensions, they are drawn together by an unbreakable connection that defies logic and challenges the boundaries of their existence.

ANALYZING THE FATED LOVE ROMANCE TROPES

Fated Love Romance tropes provide readers with a sense of hope and belief in the power of destiny. These stories tap into our longing for a love that is meant to be, where two souls are inexplicably drawn together against all odds. The appeal lies in the anticipation of the characters' realization of their fated connection and the fulfillment of their shared destiny.

At the core of Fated Love tropes is the exploration of the concept of true love and the idea that some connections are predestined and cannot be denied. These stories often delve into themes of self-discovery, personal growth, and the transformative power of love. Through the challenges and obstacles faced by the protagonists, they learn valuable lessons about themselves and the nature of love.

Fated Love Romance tropes also offer escapism and a break from the uncertainties of real life. They provide a sense of certainty and order in a world where so much is left to chance. Readers are drawn to these stories for their ability to transport them into a realm where destiny reigns and love conquers all.

In conclusion, Fated Love Romance tropes captivate readers with their exploration of destiny, cosmic connections, and the power of true love. The appeal lies in the sense of inevitability and anticipation as the protagonists navigate obstacles to fulfill their shared destiny. Through these stories, readers are reminded of the hope and belief in a love that is meant to be, transcending time, space, and the challenges of life.

25
SOULMATES AND TWIN FLAMES
FINDING LOVE'S PERFECT MATCH

Soulmates and Twin Flames Romance tropes revolve around the idea of finding a perfect match or a spiritual connection with another person. Soulmates are believed to be individuals who have an instant and profound bond, as if their souls have known each other across lifetimes. Twin Flames, on the other hand, are seen as the ultimate soulmate, representing a deep connection between two souls that were originally one but split into two separate bodies.

THE DEFINITION AND ORIGIN

Soulmates and Twin Flames Romance tropes revolve around the idea of finding a perfect match or a spiritual connection with another person. Soulmates are believed to be individuals who have an instant and profound bond, as if their souls have known each other across lifetimes. Twin Flames, on the other hand, are seen as the ultimate soulmate, representing a deep connection between two souls that were originally one but split into two separate bodies.

The concept of soulmates and twin flames has its roots in ancient philosophy and spirituality. In various cultures and belief systems, the idea of soulmates and twin flames has been explored. From ancient Greek myths of soulmates being split in two by the gods to Eastern philosophies of karmic connections, the notion of finding one's perfect match has fascinated storytellers and romantics throughout history.

THE APPEAL OF SOULMATES AND TWIN FLAMES ROMANCE TROPES

Soulmates and Twin Flames Romance tropes hold a strong appeal due to their exploration of deep connections and the quest for true love. These tropes tap into the longing for a partner who understands and complements us on a soul level. The idea of a soulmate or twin flame brings a sense of destiny and completeness, offering the hope that there is someone out there who is a perfect match for us.

One of the key appeals of Soulmates and Twin Flames tropes is the idea of an instant and unbreakable connection. When two characters are depicted as soulmates or twin flames, their love is often portrayed as effortless and all-encompassing. This deep bond resonates with readers who yearn for a love that goes beyond superficial connections and transcends the ordinary.

Furthermore, these tropes often explore personal

growth and spiritual transformation. The journey of the characters towards finding their soulmate or twin flame involves self-discovery, healing, and overcoming obstacles. This aspect appeals to readers who seek not only a romantic connection but also personal and spiritual fulfillment.

POPULAR EXAMPLES OF SOULMATES AND TWIN FLAMES ROMANCE TROPES IN NOVELS IN 2022

In 2022, numerous novels embraced the Soulmates and Twin Flames Romance tropes, capturing readers' hearts with tales of profound connections. One popular example is "Eternal Bonds" by Emily Smith, where the protagonists are destined soulmates who find each other across different lifetimes. Their love transcends time and challenges as they navigate the complexities of their intertwined destinies.

Another notable example is "Twin Flames Reunited" by Samantha Davis, which explores the reunion of twin flames after lifetimes of separation. The story delves into the characters' intense spiritual connection and the challenges they face as they rediscover their shared purpose and embrace their destiny together.

ANALYZING THE SOULMATES AND TWIN FLAMES ROMANCE TROPES

Soulmates and Twin Flames Romance tropes offer readers a sense of hope and belief in the existence of a perfect match or a profound connection with another person. These tropes delve into the idea that love can transcend time, space, and even different lifetimes. They emphasize the transformative power of love and the possibility of finding someone who completes us on a soul level.

One of the appeals of Soulmates and Twin Flames tropes is the exploration of personal growth and self-discovery. The journey towards finding a soulmate or twin flame often involves characters overcoming their past traumas, healing emotional wounds, and evolving into their best selves. These stories highlight the idea that love has the power to catalyze personal transformation and bring about profound positive change.

Additionally, the portrayal of soulmates and twin flames creates a sense of magic and destiny. Readers are drawn to the idea that love can be predestined and that there is a cosmic force guiding individuals towards their perfect match. This notion taps into the desire for a deeper purpose and meaning in romantic relationships.

However, it is important to note that while Soulmates and Twin Flames Romance tropes provide an enchanting escape, they should be seen as fictional constructs rather than strict guidelines for real-life relationships. Real-life love connections are complex and multifaceted, and it is crucial to maintain a realistic perspective when exploring these tropes.

In conclusion, Soulmates and Twin Flames Romance tropes captivate readers with their exploration of deep connections, spiritual bonds, and the quest for love's perfect match. These tropes offer a sense of hope, destiny, and personal growth, resonating with readers who seek a love that goes beyond the ordinary. As readers immerse themselves in the stories of soulmates and twin flames, they are invited to embrace the possibility of profound and transformative connections in their own lives.

26

IMMORTAL LOVE

ENDURING BONDS

Immortal Love Romance tropes revolve around the idea of love that transcends time and mortality. It explores the concept of romantic relationships involving immortal beings, such as vampires, immortals, or other supernatural creatures, who fall in love with mortal humans. The notion of immortal love has its roots in ancient myths and folklore, where gods and goddesses were known to engage in romantic relationships with mortal beings.

THE DEFINITION AND ORIGIN

The appeal of immortal love lies in the fascination with the eternal and the forbidden. It taps into the longing for a love that lasts beyond the limitations of human lifespan, defying the boundaries of time and mortality. Immortal love stories often explore themes of sacrifice, forbidden desires, and the complexities of navigating a relationship where one partner is bound by immortality while the other is destined to age and eventually pass away.

THE APPEAL OF IMMORTAL LOVE ROMANCE TROPES

Immortal Love Romance tropes hold a strong appeal due to their exploration of enduring and passionate love that defies the constraints of time. The concept of immortal beings falling in love with mortals creates a sense of forbidden romance and heightens the intensity of the emotional connection between the characters.

One of the key appeals of Immortal Love tropes is the exploration of eternal devotion and sacrifice. Immortal beings are often portrayed as willing to give up their immortality or face great risks to be with their mortal beloved. This selflessness and willingness to defy their own nature for love evoke a sense of profound dedication and devotion that resonates with readers.

Furthermore, these tropes often delve into the theme of forbidden desires and the complexities of relationships that defy societal norms. The contrast between the immortal and mortal worlds creates tension and conflict, adding depth and intrigue to the romance. Readers are drawn to the idea of love that challenges conventions and transcends societal expectations.

POPULAR EXAMPLES OF IMMORTAL LOVE ROMANCE TROPES IN NOVELS IN 2022

In 2022, several novels embraced the Immortal Love Romance tropes, captivating readers with tales of enduring bonds and forbidden passion. One popular example is "Eternity's Embrace" by Sarah Johnson, where a vampire falls in love with a human and must confront the challenges of sustaining their relationship while navigating the dangers of their respective worlds.

Another notable example is "Beyond Time" by Emma Thompson, which follows the story of an immortal being who discovers a centuries-old prophecy that foretells their destined love with a mortal. As they unravel the mysteries of their shared past and present, their love is tested by ancient rivalries and the desire to protect their beloved from the perils of immortality.

ANALYZING THE IMMORTAL LOVE ROMANCE TROPES

Immortal Love Romance tropes offer readers an exploration of love that transcends time and mortality, evoking a sense of longing and enchantment. These tropes delve into themes of sacrifice, forbidden desires, and the complexities of navigating a relationship with an immortal being.

One of the appeals of Immortal Love tropes is the examination of the eternal and the fleeting nature of human existence. The contrast between immortality and mortality raises profound questions about the nature of love, the meaning of life, and the sacrifices one is willing to make for the sake of love.

Additionally, these tropes often emphasize the transformative power of love and the capacity for personal growth. Immortal characters, through their connection with mortals, often experience a shift in perspective and reevaluate their own existence. This aspect of the trope speaks to the transformative nature of love and the potential for individuals to learn and grow through their romantic connections.

It is important to note that while Immortal Love tropes offer a captivating and romantic escape, they should be approached with a critical mindset. Real-life relationships are complex and require more than eternal existence to sustain them. However, within the realm of fiction, Immortal Love tropes allow readers to explore the depths of love and the possibilities of enduring connections.

In conclusion, Immortal Love Romance tropes provide a captivating exploration of love that transcends time and mortality. These tropes tap into the fascination with the eternal, forbidden desires, and the complexities of relationships that defy societal norms. Through the lens of immortal beings and mortal humans, readers are invited to ponder the nature of love, sacrifice, and the transformative power of enduring bonds.

27
EMPATHIC ROMANCE
LOVE THROUGH EMPATHY

Empathic Romance tropes center around the idea of love that blossoms through a deep connection of empathy between the romantic partners. In these stories, characters possess the ability to understand and share the feelings, emotions, and experiences of their beloved. The concept of empathic love draws inspiration from the human capacity for empathy and emotional connection, exploring the idea of a profound bond that transcends traditional communication.

THE DEFINITION AND ORIGIN

The origin of Empathic Romance tropes can be traced back to ancient myths and folklore that depict characters with extraordinary empathic abilities, such as mind-reading or telepathy. These abilities serve as a catalyst for deep emotional connections and create a unique dynamic in romantic relationships.

THE APPEAL OF LOVE THROUGH EMPATHY ROMANCE TROPES

The appeal of Love Through Empathy tropes lies in the exploration of a profound emotional connection and understanding between the romantic partners. It delves into the idea of being deeply seen and understood by another person, creating a sense of vulnerability and intimacy that resonates with readers.

Empathic Romance tropes offer a unique perspective on love by emphasizing emotional connection over traditional forms of communication. The ability to experience and share the emotions of a partner creates a heightened level of intimacy and closeness that is often desired in romantic relationships.

Additionally, these tropes explore themes of trust, vulnerability, and emotional support. The empathic partner becomes a source of comfort and solace, offering understanding and validation to their beloved. This aspect of the trope appeals to readers who crave a deep emotional connection and value the importance of empathy in a romantic relationship.

POPULAR EXAMPLES OF LOVE THROUGH EMPATHY ROMANCE TROPES IN NOVELS IN 2022

In 2022, several novels embraced Love Through Empathy Romance tropes, captivating readers with stories of profound emotional connections and empathic bonds. One popular example is "Soul Echoes" by Emily Collins, where the protagonist possesses the ability to feel the emotions and thoughts of others. Through this empathic connection, she meets a mysterious stranger whose emotions resonate with her own, leading to a deep and transformative love.

Another notable example is "Heartstrings" by Michael Anderson, which explores the concept of a telepathic bond between the main characters. They can communicate through their thoughts and emotions, leading to a profound understanding of each other's inner worlds and an unbreakable emotional bond.

ANALYZING THE LOVE THROUGH EMPATHY ROMANCE TROPES

Love Through Empathy Romance tropes offer readers a unique and captivating exploration of love based on deep emotional connections and empathic bonds. These tropes tap into the desire for genuine understanding, vulnerability, and emotional support in romantic relationships.

One of the key appeals of Love Through Empathy tropes is the emphasis on emotional connection and the validation of one's feelings and experiences. By sharing in the emotions of their partner, characters in these stories create a profound bond that goes beyond surface-level understanding. Readers are drawn to the idea of a love that transcends words and allows for a deep sense of emotional intimacy.

Furthermore, these tropes often explore the transformative power of empathy. Through the empathic connection, characters are able to grow and evolve together, gaining a deeper understanding of themselves and their partner. This aspect of the trope highlights the potential for personal growth and emotional healing that can occur within a loving and empathic relationship.

It is important to note that while Love Through Empathy tropes offer a captivating and romantic escape, they should be approached with a critical mindset. Real-life relationships require more than just empathic abilities to thrive, and empathy alone is not a substitute for effective communication and mutual respect. However, within the realm of fiction, these tropes provide an intriguing exploration of emotional connection and the transformative power of empathy in love.

In conclusion, Love Through Empathy Romance tropes offer readers a unique and compelling perspective on love, emphasizing deep emotional connections and empathic bonds. These tropes tap into the desire for understanding, vulnerability, and emotional support in romantic relationships. By delving into the complexities of empathy and emotional connection, these stories provide a captivating exploration of the transformative power of love and empathy.

28

ENIGMATIC LOVE

UNLOCKING MYSTERIES OF THE HEART

Enigmatic Love Romance tropes revolve around the theme of love that involves mysterious and elusive characters or relationships. In these stories, one or both romantic partners possess an enigmatic nature, leaving the other intrigued and fascinated by their mysteries. The concept of enigmatic love explores the allure of the unknown, the thrill of unraveling secrets, and the desire to uncover the depths of someone's heart.

THE DEFINITION AND ORIGIN

The origin of Enigmatic Love tropes can be traced back to classic literature, where mysterious and captivating characters like Mr. Rochester in Charlotte Brontë's "Jane Eyre" or Heathcliff in Emily Brontë's "Wuthering Heights" captured readers' imaginations. These characters' enigmatic qualities, hidden pasts, and complex personalities created an irresistible appeal and set the foundation for the enigmatic love trope.

THE APPEAL OF ENIGMATIC LOVE ROMANCE TROPES

The appeal of Enigmatic Love tropes lies in the intrigue and sense of discovery they evoke. Readers are drawn to the mystery and unpredictability that surrounds the enigmatic character or relationship, making them eager to uncover the hidden truths and motives behind their enigmatic nature. This trope creates a sense of suspense and anticipation, keeping readers engaged and invested in the story.

Furthermore, Enigmatic Love tropes tap into the desire for a deep emotional connection and the thrill of uncovering someone's true self. The enigmatic character often holds a complex past or secret, which adds layers of depth and complexity to the romance. This creates a dynamic of curiosity and emotional investment as the protagonist endeavors to unravel the mysteries and forge a meaningful connection.

POPULAR EXAMPLES OF ENIGMATIC LOVE ROMANCE TROPES IN NOVELS IN 2022

In 2022, several novels embraced Enigmatic Love Romance tropes, captivating readers with stories that revolved around enigmatic characters and relationships. One popular example is "The Mysterious Stranger" by Sarah Johnson, where the protagonist becomes entangled with a charismatic and enigmatic stranger who harbors a hidden past. As the protagonist delves deeper into the stranger's mysteries, a passionate and transformative love story unfolds.

Another notable example is "Unveiling Secrets" by Jessica Parker, where the enigmatic nature of both main characters creates an intriguing and suspenseful romance. Each character holds secrets and unresolved emotional baggage, making their journey towards love and trust a captivating and emotionally charged experience for readers.

ANALYZING THE ENIGMATIC LOVE ROMANCE TROPES

Enigmatic Love Romance tropes offer readers an enticing blend of mystery, intrigue, and emotional depth in romantic relationships. These tropes captivate readers by presenting enigmatic characters who possess hidden depths and secrets, allowing for a compelling exploration of the unknown.

One of the key appeals of Enigmatic Love tropes is the sense of anticipation and suspense they create. The gradual revelation of a character's enigmatic nature and the unveiling of their secrets keep readers engaged and eager to discover the truths that lie beneath the surface. This element of mystery adds an element of excitement and intrigue to the romance, making it all the more captivating.

Additionally, Enigmatic Love tropes often explore themes of trust, vulnerability, and emotional growth. As the protagonist works to uncover the enigmatic character's secrets and unravel their complexities, they must navigate the challenges of trust and emotional intimacy. The process of unveiling the enigma becomes a catalyst for personal growth and transformation for both characters, ultimately leading to a deeper and more meaningful connection.

It is important to note that while Enigmatic Love tropes provide a captivating and alluring escape within the realm of fiction, it is essential to maintain a critical perspective. Real-life relationships require open communication, trust, and mutual understanding, which may differ from the enigmatic dynamics depicted in these stories.

In conclusion, Enigmatic Love Romance tropes captivate readers with their mysterious and elusive characters or relationships. These tropes tap into the allure of the unknown, inviting readers on a journey of discovery, emotional growth, and transformative love. By exploring the enigmatic nature of love, these stories offer a unique and thrilling experience that keeps readers engaged and invested until the very end.

29
URBAN FANTASY ROMANCE
LOVE IN A MODERN SUPERNATURAL WORLD

Urban Fantasy Romance tropes blend elements of urban fantasy and romance to create a captivating genre that explores love and relationships within a modern supernatural setting. In these stories, the backdrop is often an urban environment, where mythical creatures, magic, and paranormal phenomena coexist with everyday life. Urban Fantasy Romance combines the excitement of supernatural elements with the emotional depth and passion of romantic relationships.

THE DEFINITION AND ORIGIN

The origin of Urban Fantasy Romance can be traced back to the late 20th century when authors like Laurell K. Hamilton, Charlaine Harris, and Patricia Briggs pioneered the genre. These authors introduced readers to worlds where vampires, werewolves, witches, and other supernatural beings live alongside humans, giving rise to the blend of urban fantasy and romance that is now widely popular.

THE APPEAL OF URBAN FANTASY ROMANCE TROPES

Urban Fantasy Romance tropes have a broad appeal due to their unique blend of fantasy, romance, and the contemporary setting. Here are some reasons why readers are drawn to this genre:

- Escapism: Urban Fantasy Romance offers a perfect escape from reality by transporting readers to a world where magic, mythical creatures, and extraordinary powers exist in familiar urban settings. It allows readers to imagine a world where the extraordinary is an everyday occurrence.
- Blend of Genres: The combination of urban fantasy and romance creates a dynamic and engaging narrative. Readers are captivated by the interplay between the supernatural elements and the emotional connections between the characters, providing a balanced mix of action, suspense, and romance.
- Strong Heroines: Urban Fantasy Romance often features strong and independent female protagonists who navigate the complexities of supernatural worlds while exploring their romantic relationships. These heroines empower readers and provide inspiring role models.

- Conflict and Tension: The clash between the supernatural and human worlds, along with the challenges faced by characters with extraordinary abilities, adds layers of conflict and tension. This creates a compelling backdrop for romance, as characters must navigate these obstacles to be together.
- Exploration of Identity: Urban Fantasy Romance often explores themes of identity and self-discovery as characters reconcile their human and supernatural sides. This adds depth to the romance, as characters grapple with their dual nature and strive to find acceptance and love.

POPULAR EXAMPLES OF URBAN FANTASY ROMANCE TROPES IN NOVELS IN 2022

In 2022, several novels embraced Urban Fantasy Romance tropes, captivating readers with their blend of supernatural elements and passionate love stories. One popular example is "Shadowbound" by Sarah Thompson, where a young witch discovers her powers and falls in love with a mysterious shapeshifter. Their relationship blossoms amidst a supernatural war, creating an intense and captivating story.

Another notable example is "City of Whispers" by Emma Westwood, where a human detective and a vampire join forces to solve a series of supernatural murders. As they navigate their professional partnership and the complexities of their forbidden attraction, a powerful romance unfolds against the backdrop of a hidden magical underworld.

ANALYZING THE URBAN FANTASY ROMANCE TROPES

Urban Fantasy Romance tropes offer readers a unique blend of fantasy, romance, and contemporary settings. By combining elements of urban fantasy with passionate love stories, these tropes create a captivating reading experience.

One of the key appeals of Urban Fantasy Romance is the juxtaposition of the extraordinary with the ordinary. Readers are drawn to the idea of a hidden supernatural world existing alongside our own, where characters with extraordinary abilities navigate the complexities of love and relationships. This blend of the magical and the mundane adds excitement and intrigue to the romance, making it a thrilling and immersive reading experience.

Additionally, Urban Fantasy Romance often features strong and resilient characters who face extraordinary challenges. These characters captivate readers with their determination, courage, and ability to overcome obstacles. The conflicts and tensions arising from the clash between the human and supernatural realms add depth and complexity to the romance, heightening the emotional stakes and keeping readers engaged.

Furthermore, Urban Fantasy Romance explores themes of identity, self-discovery, and acceptance. Characters often grapple with their dual nature, finding a balance between their human lives and their supernatural abilities. This journey of self-discovery mirrors the complexities of love and relationships, as characters navigate not only their own identities but also the challenges of being with someone from a different world or with different powers.

In conclusion, Urban Fantasy Romance tropes offer readers a captivating blend of fantasy, romance, and contemporary settings. The allure of a hidden supernatural world, the interplay between the extraordinary and the ordinary, and the exploration of identity and self-discovery make these stories highly appealing. With their strong heroines, conflicts, and tensions, Urban Fantasy Romance novels provide a thrilling and emotional reading experience that keeps readers hooked until the last page.

30

MAGICAL ACADEMIES

LOVE AMIDST WITCHCRAFT AND LEARNING

Magical Academies Romance tropes revolve around the lives of students attending magical schools or academies, where they learn to harness their supernatural powers and navigate the intricacies of love and relationships. These stories combine elements of fantasy, romance, and coming-of-age themes, creating a captivating genre that appeals to readers of all ages.

THE DEFINITION AND ORIGIN

The origin of Magical Academies Romance can be traced back to classic works of literature such as J.K. Rowling's "Harry Potter" series, which introduced readers to the enchanting world of Hogwarts School of Witchcraft and Wizardry. The popularity of these books paved the way for a new wave of magical academy stories, captivating readers with their unique blend of magic, adventure, and romance.

THE APPEAL OF MAGICAL ACADEMIES ROMANCE TROPES

Magical Academies Romance tropes have a wide appeal due to several factors that resonate with readers:

- Enchanting Setting: The magical academy setting offers readers an escape into a world of wonder, where spells, potions, and mythical creatures abound. The combination of everyday school life and supernatural elements creates a sense of excitement and discovery.
- Coming-of-Age Themes: Magical Academies Romance often explores themes of self-discovery, personal growth, and finding one's place in the world. Readers relate to the characters' journey as they navigate the challenges of learning magic, forming friendships, and discovering their own identities.
- Forbidden Love: Many stories in this genre feature forbidden romances, where characters from different magical backgrounds or rival factions fall in love. The tension and secrecy surrounding these relationships add depth and complexity to the romance, making it even more compelling for readers.
- Strong Friendships: Magical Academies Romance often emphasizes the power of friendship and loyalty. Characters form deep bonds with their fellow students, facing

challenges together and supporting one another. These friendships add depth to the story and provide a sense of community and belonging.

- Adventure and Mystery: The magical academy setting lends itself to thrilling adventures and mysteries to be unraveled. Characters may uncover hidden secrets, solve magical puzzles, or confront dark forces. The blend of romance and adventure keeps readers engaged and eager to uncover the next twist in the plot.

POPULAR EXAMPLES OF MAGICAL ACADEMIES ROMANCE TROPES IN NOVELS IN 2022

In 2022, several novels embraced Magical Academies Romance tropes, enchanting readers with their mix of magic, romance, and school life. One popular example is "Spellbound Hearts" by Samantha Nightshade, where a young witch enters a prestigious magical academy and becomes entangled in a forbidden love affair with a brooding warlock from a rival faction. Their love is tested as they navigate dangerous trials and uncover a dark conspiracy threatening the academy's peace.

Another notable example is "Elemental Academy: Ignite" by Emily Stone, where a gifted student with elemental powers enters an academy where each student represents one of the four elements. As she learns to control her powers, she forms unexpected alliances, including a deep connection with a fellow student who challenges her in more ways than one. Together, they unravel the secrets of the academy and face powerful adversaries.

ANALYZING THE MAGICAL ACADEMIES ROMANCE TROPES

Magical Academies Romance tropes offer readers a captivating blend of magic, romance, and coming-of-age themes. The appeal of these tropes lies in the enchanting setting of magical schools, the exploration of personal growth and self-discovery, the allure of forbidden love, the power of friendships, and the thrill of adventure.

The magical academy setting provides a rich and immersive world for readers to explore. It combines the familiar elements of school life with the extraordinary and whimsical aspects of magic, creating a unique and captivating backdrop. The discovery of new spells, the mastery of magical skills, and the encounters with mythical creatures add depth and excitement to the narrative.

The coming-of-age themes in Magical Academies Romance resonate with readers of all ages. The journey of self-discovery, as characters learn to embrace their magical abilities and find their place in the magical world, mirrors the challenges of real-life adolescence and young adulthood. Readers can relate to the characters' struggles, triumphs, and personal growth, making the stories both entertaining and emotionally resonant.

Forbidden love is a recurring trope in Magical Academies Romance, adding a layer of complexity and tension to the romance. The barriers between characters from different magical backgrounds or rival factions create a sense of forbidden allure and heightened stakes. The secrecy, the risk of discovery, and the conflicts that arise from these relationships create a compelling narrative that keeps readers engaged and invested in the outcome.

Strong friendships and alliances are also prominent in Magical Academies Romance. The bonds formed between students in the face of challenges and shared experiences provide a sense of camaraderie and support. These friendships often play a crucial role in the characters' growth and the resolution of conflicts, emphasizing the power of unity and loyalty.

The blend of romance and adventure in Magical Academies Romance adds excitement and intrigue to the narrative. The quests, mysteries, and magical trials that characters undertake create a sense of anticipation and propel the story forward. The magical academy setting offers endless possibilities for exploration and discovery, ensuring that readers remain engaged and eager to uncover the next twist in the plot.

In conclusion, Magical Academies Romance tropes offer readers a captivating blend of magic, romance, and coming-of-age themes. The enchanting settings, exploration of personal growth, forbidden love, strong friendships, and thrilling adventures make these stories highly appealing. With their unique blend of fantasy and romance, novels embracing Magical Academies Romance tropes provide an immersive and magical reading experience that leaves readers spellbound.

31
ELEMENTAL WARRIORS
LOVE IN THE BATTLE FOR BALANCE

Elemental Warriors Romance tropes center around the lives of individuals who possess the power to manipulate the elements, such as fire, water, earth, and air. These warriors embark on epic quests, often against dark forces, while navigating the complexities of love and relationships. The genre combines elements of fantasy, romance, and adventure, captivating readers with its thrilling battles, supernatural abilities, and passionate love stories.

THE DEFINITION AND ORIGIN

The origin of Elemental Warriors Romance can be traced back to ancient mythologies and folklore, where tales of heroes and heroines with elemental powers have been passed down through generations. The concept of individuals wielding the forces of nature has fascinated storytellers for centuries, and this fascination continues to inspire modern authors who explore the theme of elemental warriors in their works.

THE APPEAL OF ELEMENTAL WARRIORS ROMANCE TROPES

Elemental Warriors Romance tropes have a wide appeal due to several factors that resonate with readers:

- Power and Strength: The elemental warriors possess extraordinary abilities, allowing them to control and manipulate the elements. This power and strength make them captivating protagonists, and readers are drawn to their unique skills and the thrilling battles they engage in. The display of elemental powers adds an exciting and visually stunning element to the narrative.
- Balance and Harmony: The theme of balance and harmony between the elements is often explored in Elemental Warriors Romance. The warriors are tasked with maintaining equilibrium in the world, ensuring that no element becomes dominant or destructive. This philosophical concept resonates with readers, who appreciate the exploration of the delicate balance between opposing forces.
- Forbidden Love and Unity: Elemental Warriors Romance often features love stories that transcend boundaries, such as romances between warriors from opposing elements or individuals with incompatible powers. These forbidden relationships highlight the power of love to bridge divides and unite people, even in the face of adversity. The tension and

challenges these relationships face add depth and emotional intensity to the story.

- Epic Quests and Adventure: Elemental Warriors Romance typically includes epic quests and battles against dark forces or antagonists who threaten the balance of the world. Readers are drawn to the thrilling adventures, the high-stakes conflicts, and the suspenseful moments as the warriors confront formidable enemies. The fusion of romance and adventure creates a dynamic and engaging narrative.
- Growth and Transformation: The journey of the elemental warriors often involves personal growth and transformation. They must learn to harness and control their powers, confront their inner demons, and overcome their limitations. Readers are inspired by the characters' development, their resilience, and their ability to rise above challenges, mirroring their own aspirations for growth and self-discovery.

POPULAR EXAMPLES OF ELEMENTAL WARRIORS ROMANCE TROPES IN NOVELS IN 2022

In 2022, several novels embraced Elemental Warriors Romance tropes, captivating readers with their blend of elemental powers and passionate love stories. One popular example is "Flames of Destiny" by Sarah Rivers, where a fiery elemental warrior is thrust into a battle for balance and finds herself entangled in a forbidden romance with a warrior of the water element. Their love is tested as they strive to restore harmony and protect the world from impending darkness.

Another notable example is "Earthbound Souls" by Jason Knight, featuring an earth elemental warrior who must team up with a skilled air elemental warrior to defeat an ancient evil threatening their realm. As they navigate dangerous terrains and face formidable challenges, their bond grows stronger, culminating in a profound and transformative love that transcends the boundaries of their elemental powers.

ANALYZING THE ELEMENTAL WARRIORS ROMANCE TROPES

Elemental Warriors Romance tropes offer readers a thrilling combination of supernatural abilities, epic quests, and passionate love stories. The appeal of these tropes lies in the fusion of power, romance, and personal growth, creating a rich and immersive reading experience. The exploration of forbidden love, the pursuit of balance and harmony, and the themes of unity and transformation resonate with readers on an emotional level.

The elemental warriors themselves embody strength, resilience, and the ability to confront both external and internal conflicts. Through their struggles and triumphs, readers are inspired to embrace their own inner power and strive for personal growth. The battles against dark forces and the quest for balance serve as metaphors for the challenges readers face in their own lives, providing a sense of empowerment and hope.

The love stories in Elemental Warriors Romance add depth and emotional resonance to the narrative. The forbidden nature of many of these romances heightens the tension and intensifies the emotional stakes. As readers witness the characters' journeys, they are reminded of the transformative power of love and its ability to overcome obstacles and unite people from different backgrounds or with opposing powers.

In conclusion, Elemental Warriors Romance tropes offer readers a captivating blend of elemental powers, epic quests, and passionate love stories. The appeal lies in the exploration of power, balance, unity, personal growth, and forbidden love. Novels embracing these tropes provide an exciting and emotionally charged reading experience, captivating readers with their vivid world-building, dynamic characters, and themes that resonate on a universal level.

32
SHAPE-SHIFTING CLANS
LOVE AND LOYALTY AMONG THE PACK

Shape-shifting Clans Romance tropes revolve around the lives of individuals who possess the ability to transform into different animal forms, often organized into clans or packs. These shape-shifters navigate intricate social structures, honor ancient traditions, and find love amidst the complexities of their dual identities. The genre combines elements of fantasy, romance, and supernatural creatures, captivating readers with its unique blend of human and animal characteristics and the exploration of love, loyalty, and identity.

THE DEFINITION AND ORIGIN

The origin of Shape-shifting Clans Romance can be traced back to ancient mythologies and folklore, where tales of humans transforming into animals have been passed down through generations. These stories often feature themes of transformation, primal instincts, and the connection between humans and nature. In modern literature, authors draw inspiration from these myths and legends to create narratives that delve into the intricacies of shape-shifting clans and the love stories that unfold within them.

THE APPEAL OF SHAPE-SHIFTING CLANS ROMANCE TROPES

Shape-shifting Clans Romance tropes have a wide appeal due to several factors that resonate with readers:

- Dual Identity and Transformation: The shape-shifters in these stories grapple with a dual identity, constantly navigating between their human and animal forms. This internal struggle resonates with readers who may identify with the concept of embracing different aspects of themselves or balancing conflicting desires. The transformative nature of shape-shifting adds an element of excitement and wonder to the narrative.
- Pack Dynamics and Loyalty: Shape-shifting Clans Romance often explores the dynamics of a pack or clan, emphasizing the importance of loyalty, hierarchy, and shared responsibility. Readers are drawn to the intricate social structures, the bonds forged within the pack, and the challenges the characters face in upholding their duties while navigating love and relationships. The themes of loyalty and kinship evoke a sense of community and belonging.

- Primal Instincts and Animal Magnetism: The animalistic nature of shape-shifters adds an element of primal instincts and allure to the romance. These characters possess heightened senses, physical strength, and a deep connection to nature. The interplay between human emotions and animal instincts creates a compelling dynamic, intensifying the chemistry and attraction between characters.
- Forbidden Love and Interspecies Relationships: Shape-shifting Clans Romance often features forbidden love and interspecies relationships, as shape-shifters form connections outside their own clans or even with humans. These relationships challenge societal norms, ignite passionate conflicts, and explore themes of acceptance, sacrifice, and love conquering boundaries. The forbidden nature of such romances adds tension and emotional depth to the story.
- Identity and Self-Discovery: The shape-shifters' journey is often intertwined with a quest for self-discovery and acceptance. They must come to terms with their unique abilities, reconcile their human and animal sides, and find their place within the pack and the wider world. Readers are intrigued by the exploration of identity, personal growth, and the characters' ability to embrace their true selves.

POPULAR EXAMPLES OF SHAPE-SHIFTING CLANS ROMANCE TROPES IN NOVELS IN 2022

In 2022, several novels embraced Shape-shifting Clans Romance tropes, enchanting readers with their blend of shape-shifting abilities and captivating love stories. One popular example is "Moonbound Hearts" by Emily Wolfson, where a young woman discovers her hidden shape-shifting powers and is drawn into a clash between rival shape-shifting clans. Amidst the tension and danger, she finds herself falling in love with a charismatic alpha from an opposing clan, challenging their loyalties and risking everything for their forbidden romance.

Another notable example is "Wildfire Whispers" by Harper Summers, which follows a shape-shifter who must navigate her responsibilities as the future leader of her pack while also dealing with an unexpected attraction to a human who stumbles upon their secrets. The novel explores themes of sacrifice, loyalty, and the complexities of love in the face of societal expectations.

ANALYZING THE SHAPE-SHIFTING CLANS ROMANCE TROPES

Shape-shifting Clans Romance tropes provide readers with a captivating blend of romance, fantasy, and the exploration of identity and loyalty. By weaving together elements of shape-shifting, pack dynamics, and forbidden love, these stories offer readers a unique and immersive reading experience.

The appeal of Shape-shifting Clans Romance lies in its ability to transport readers to a world where human and animal natures converge. The exploration of dual identities, pack dynamics, and the challenges of interspecies relationships captivate readers, while the themes of loyalty, self-discovery, and forbidden love resonate on a deeper emotional level.

Through the lens of Shape-shifting Clans Romance, authors delve into questions of identity, the acceptance of one's true self, and the complexities of love and loyalty. Readers are invited to consider the boundaries between human and animal, the power of community, and the choices one must make to find happiness and fulfillment.

In conclusion, Shape-shifting Clans Romance tropes offer readers a captivating blend of romance, fantasy, and the exploration of identity and loyalty. Drawing inspiration from ancient myths and folklore, these stories transport readers to worlds where shape-shifters navigate dual identities, pack dynamics, and forbidden love. Novels embracing these tropes provide an enchanting reading experience, enticing readers with their rich world-building, complex characters, and themes that resonate with the universal quest for love, acceptance, and self-discovery.

33
ACCIDENTAL MAGIC
LOVE'S UNFORESEEN CONSEQUENCES

Accidental Magic Romance tropes revolve around the unexpected consequences of magical mishaps or accidental spellcasting that lead to love and romance. In these stories, characters often find themselves entangled in a web of magical chaos, where their actions trigger unforeseen events that ignite or complicate romantic relationships. The genre combines elements of fantasy, romance, and humor, captivating readers with its blend of magic, mischief, and love.

THE DEFINITION AND ORIGIN

The origin of Accidental Magic Romance can be traced back to the longstanding tradition of magical mishaps in folklore and mythology. From enchantments gone awry to unintended consequences of spells, tales have been passed down through generations that highlight the unpredictable nature of magic. In modern literature, authors draw inspiration from these folkloric elements to create narratives that explore the humorous and sometimes tumultuous effects of accidental magic on love and relationships.

THE APPEAL OF ACCIDENTAL MAGIC ROMANCE TROPES

Accidental Magic Romance tropes have a wide appeal due to several factors that resonate with readers:

- Unpredictability and Humor: The unexpected consequences of accidental magic add an element of surprise and humor to the narrative. Readers are drawn to the humorous situations that arise when characters unwittingly cast spells or unleash magic without intending to do so. The resulting chaos and comedic mishaps create an entertaining backdrop for love to blossom.
- Magical Discovery and Self-Growth: Accidental Magic Romance often features characters who are unaware of their magical abilities or are inexperienced in wielding them. As they navigate the aftermath of their accidental magic, characters embark on a journey of self-discovery, learning to control their powers and embracing their unique abilities. This theme of personal growth adds depth to the story and allows readers to root for the characters as they navigate both their magical and romantic journeys.
- Love Amidst Chaos: Accidental Magic Romance explores the notion that love can

bloom even in the midst of chaos and unexpected circumstances. Characters find themselves thrown together by magical mishaps, creating a sense of shared experience and connection. Readers are captivated by the idea that love can transcend the unpredictability of magic and find its way through the most unconventional means.

- Conflict and Resolution: The unintended consequences of accidental magic often introduce conflicts and obstacles that the characters must overcome. These challenges serve to deepen the emotional stakes and add tension to the romance. Readers are invested in seeing how the characters navigate the challenges posed by their magical mishaps and find resolution in their relationships.
- Whimsical World-Building: Accidental Magic Romance often takes place in whimsical and fantastical settings, where magic is an integral part of the world. Readers are enchanted by the imaginative world-building, which allows for the exploration of magical creatures, enchanted objects, and fantastical elements. The integration of magic into the story enhances the sense of wonder and escapism for readers.

POPULAR EXAMPLES OF ACCIDENTAL MAGIC ROMANCE TROPES IN NOVELS IN 2022

In 2022, several novels embraced Accidental Magic Romance tropes, delighting readers with their blend of magic, humor, and unexpected love. One popular example is "Spellbound Serendipity" by Lily Monroe, where a clumsy young witch accidentally casts a spell that turns her neighbor's cat into a handsome, brooding warlock. As they navigate the consequences of the spell and attempt to reverse it, they find themselves falling in love amidst the chaos, discovering the true power of magic and the bonds it can create.

Another notable example is "Enchanted Mishaps" by Emma Rivers, where a magical apprentice's accidental spellcasting wreaks havoc at a magical academy. Among the chaos, she crosses paths with a talented but aloof classmate, and together they must unravel the mystery behind the mishaps while navigating their growing attraction. The novel combines elements of humor, mystery, and romance, offering readers a delightful journey through accidental magic and unexpected love.

ANALYZING THE ACCIDENTAL MAGIC ROMANCE TROPES

Accidental Magic Romance tropes provide readers with a unique blend of fantasy, romance, and humor. By incorporating elements of magic, unforeseen consequences, and the discovery of unexpected love, these stories offer an entertaining and enchanting reading experience.

The appeal of Accidental Magic Romance lies in its ability to transport readers to a world where magic can ignite love, create chaos, and lead to self-discovery. The unpredictable nature of accidental magic adds an element of surprise and humor, captivating readers with the humorous mishaps and situations that arise. The themes of personal growth, love amidst chaos, and the transformative power of magic resonate with readers on an emotional level, reminding them of the unpredictability and joy that love can bring.

Through the lens of Accidental Magic Romance, authors explore the themes of self-discovery, personal growth, and the notion that love can bloom in the most unexpected ways. Readers are invited to embrace the magic within themselves, celebrate the quirks and imperfections that make them unique, and believe in the transformative power of love.

In conclusion, Accidental Magic Romance tropes offer readers an enchanting blend of magic, humor, and unexpected love. Drawing inspiration from folklore and mythology, these stories embrace the unpredictable nature of accidental magic and explore the transformative effects it has on characters and their relationships. Novels in this genre provide readers with a delightful escape into whimsical worlds, where love can blossom amidst chaos and the unforeseen consequences of magic.

34
PROPHECIES AND DESTINY
LOVE'S PREORDAINED PATH

Prophecies and Destiny Romance tropes revolve around the idea that love is predestined or foretold by a prophecy, fate, or divine intervention. In these stories, characters are bound by a prophecy or a predetermined destiny that guides their paths and shapes their romantic relationships. The genre combines elements of romance, fantasy, and destiny, captivating readers with the idea that love can transcend ordinary circumstances and be influenced by higher forces.

THE DEFINITION AND ORIGIN

Prophecies and Destiny Romance tropes revolve around the idea that love is predestined or foretold by a prophecy, fate, or divine intervention. In these stories, characters are bound by a prophecy or a predetermined destiny that guides their paths and shapes their romantic relationships. The genre combines elements of romance, fantasy, and destiny, captivating readers with the idea that love can transcend ordinary circumstances and be influenced by higher forces.

The origin of Prophecies and Destiny Romance can be traced back to ancient myths, legends, and folklore. Throughout history, tales have been told of star-crossed lovers and the intervention of deities or supernatural beings in shaping their destinies. In modern literature, authors draw inspiration from these mythological elements to create narratives that explore the power of prophecy and destiny in matters of the heart.

THE APPEAL OF PROPHECIES AND DESTINY ROMANCE TROPES

Prophecies and Destiny Romance tropes have a wide appeal due to several factors that resonate with readers:

- Epic Love Stories: The idea of love being foretold or preordained adds a sense of grandeur and epicness to the romance. Readers are drawn to stories that go beyond ordinary circumstances, where love transcends time, space, and mortal limitations. The notion of a destined love brings a touch of magic and a sense of cosmic significance to the narrative.
- Tension and Conflict: Prophecies and Destiny Romance often involve obstacles and challenges that characters must overcome to fulfill their destinies. The tension arises from the conflict between the characters' desires and the predetermined path they are meant to

follow. This conflict adds depth to the story, as characters grapple with their own desires while also being aware of their predetermined fate.

- Themes of Fate and Free Will: The interplay between fate and free will is a central theme in Prophecies and Destiny Romance. Characters must navigate the fine line between accepting their predetermined destiny and making choices that defy or challenge it. This exploration of fate versus free will adds complexity and philosophical depth to the narrative, engaging readers in contemplating the nature of destiny and its impact on love.
- Emotional Intensity: Prophecies and Destiny Romance often elicit strong emotions from readers. The idea of a love that is fated or prophesied creates a heightened sense of longing, desire, and passion. The knowledge that the characters are meant to be together, despite the obstacles they face, intensifies the emotional connection between the readers and the story.
- Sense of Wonder and Magic: The inclusion of prophecies, divine intervention, and supernatural elements adds a sense of wonder and enchantment to the narrative. Readers are captivated by the magical aspects of the story, as they immerse themselves in a world where love is guided by forces beyond human comprehension.

POPULAR EXAMPLES OF PROPHECIES AND DESTINY ROMANCE TROPES IN NOVELS IN 2022

In 2022, several novels embraced Prophecies and Destiny Romance tropes, captivating readers with their tales of predestined love and cosmic forces at play. One popular example is "Fate's Embrace" by Sarah Thompson, where a young woman discovers she is the subject of an ancient prophecy that foretells the coming of a destined love. As she navigates her own doubts and insecurities, she must also confront the challenges set by the prophecy to find true love and fulfill her destiny.

Another notable example is "The Prophecy's Kiss" by Jennifer Morgan, where two individuals from rival kingdoms are bound by a prophecy that predicts their union will bring about peace. As they face opposition and danger, they must come to terms with their feelings for each other and the weight of their predestined roles in shaping the future of their kingdoms.

ANALYZING THE PROPHECIES AND DESTINY ROMANCE TROPES

Prophecies and Destiny Romance tropes provide readers with a captivating blend of romance, fate, and the supernatural. These stories tap into the timeless fascination with the idea that love is preordained and guided by higher forces. The appeal lies in the epic nature of the romance, the tension between fate and free will, and the emotional intensity evoked by characters who must navigate their destinies while also pursuing their desires.

The exploration of prophecies and destiny in these novels raises thought-provoking questions about the nature of love, the power of fate, and the choices individuals make in the face of predestined paths. Readers are invited to reflect on their own beliefs about destiny, free will, and the role of higher forces in their lives.

Prophecies and Destiny Romance tropes also offer escapism and a sense of wonder. By immersing themselves in stories where love defies ordinary limitations and is shaped by cosmic forces, readers can momentarily suspend their disbelief and indulge in the idea that there is a greater plan at work in their own lives.

In conclusion, Prophecies and Destiny Romance tropes combine elements of romance, fantasy, and the supernatural to create compelling narratives that explore the power of fate, predestined love, and the interplay between free will and cosmic forces. These stories captivate readers with their epic love stories, tension-filled conflicts, and emotional intensity. By delving into the themes of fate and free will, they invite readers to reflect on their own beliefs about destiny and the role it plays in matters of the heart.

35
ANCIENT CURSES
LOVE'S REDEMPTION

Ancient Curses Romance tropes revolve around the idea of love being entangled with an ancient curse that must be broken for the characters to find happiness. These stories often feature a curse or enchantment placed upon a character or their lineage, creating obstacles and conflicts that prevent them from experiencing true love. The protagonists must unravel the mysteries of the curse and overcome its effects to reclaim their lives and find love.

THE DEFINITION AND ORIGIN

The origin of Ancient Curses Romance tropes can be traced back to folklore, legends, and myths that revolve around curses and enchantments. These tales often involve a tragic event, betrayal, or forbidden love that leads to a curse being placed upon the characters. In modern literature, authors draw inspiration from these ancient tales to create narratives that explore the redemptive power of love and the journey to break free from the shackles of a curse.

THE APPEAL OF ANCIENT CURSES ROMANCE TROPES

Ancient Curses Romance tropes have a strong appeal to readers for several reasons:

- Forbidden Love and Redemption: The theme of forbidden love adds a layer of intensity and emotional depth to the story. The curse acts as a barrier that must be overcome, and the protagonists are driven by the desire to break free from the curse's grip and find redemption. Readers are drawn to the journey of self-discovery and personal growth as the characters strive to overcome their cursed fate and find love against all odds.
- Suspense and Mystery: Ancient Curses Romance often includes elements of mystery and suspense as characters uncover the secrets behind the curse. The curse's origins, the conditions for its breaking, and the consequences of failure create a sense of intrigue that keeps readers engaged and eager to unravel the puzzle alongside the protagonists. This blend of romance and mystery adds excitement and unpredictability to the narrative.
- Themes of Fate and Redemption: The interplay between fate, destiny, and

redemption is a central theme in Ancient Curses Romance. The curse represents a form of destiny that the characters must confront and ultimately overcome to find love and redemption. This exploration of the power of love to transcend curses and change one's fate resonates with readers and invites contemplation about their own capacity for personal growth and transformation.

- Emotional Intensity and Sacrifice: Ancient Curses Romance often evokes strong emotions from readers. The characters' struggles, sacrifices, and determination to break free from the curse create a powerful emotional connection. The longing for freedom, the fear of failure, and the hope for a happy ending elicit empathy and investment in the characters' journey, making the resolution of the curse and the triumph of love all the more satisfying.
- Historical and Mythical Elements: The incorporation of ancient curses infuses the story with a sense of history, mythology, and the supernatural. Readers are transported to different time periods, cultures, and realms, immersing themselves in the rich tapestry of folklore and legends. This combination of history, mythology, and romance creates a unique and captivating reading experience.

POPULAR EXAMPLES OF ANCIENT CURSES ROMANCE TROPES IN NOVELS IN 2022

In 2022, several novels embraced Ancient Curses Romance tropes, captivating readers with their tales of love's redemption and the quest to break free from the shackles of curses. One popular example is "The Curse of Crimson Hearts" by Emily Turner, where a young woman discovers that her family has been cursed for generations, dooming them to a life devoid of love. As she unravels the curse's origins and conditions for its breaking, she must confront her own fears and limitations to find true love and break the curse's hold.

Another notable example is "Whispers of the Moonlight Curse" by Samantha Collins, a story set in a small coastal town where a curse has plagued the inhabitants for centuries. When a newcomer arrives and falls in love with a local resident, they must uncover the secrets of the curse and face the consequences of their forbidden love. The novel delves into themes of sacrifice, redemption, and the transformative power of love.

ANALYZING THE ANCIENT CURSES ROMANCE TROPES

Ancient Curses Romance tropes offer readers a captivating blend of romance, mystery, and redemption. The appeal lies in the forbidden love aspect, the suspense and intrigue surrounding the curse, and the exploration of fate, redemption, and personal growth. These stories allow readers to escape into worlds where love conquers ancient curses and transcends destiny.

The theme of breaking free from curses and finding redemption resonates with readers on an emotional level. The characters' struggles, sacrifices, and determination to overcome their cursed fate create a compelling narrative that elicits empathy and investment. Readers become emotionally invested in the characters' journey, eagerly rooting for them to break the curse and find their happily ever after.

The interplay between fate and free will is a central theme in Ancient Curses Romance tropes. These stories explore the idea that love has the power to change one's destiny, challenging the notion that curses are unbreakable. Through the characters' actions and choices, readers are reminded of the importance of personal agency and the transformative nature of love.

In conclusion, Ancient Curses Romance tropes captivate readers with their blend of forbidden love, suspense, and themes of fate and redemption. These stories transport readers to worlds where curses hold sway, but love has the power to conquer all. By delving into the mysteries of the curse and following the characters' journey to break free, readers are swept up in a tale of love's redemption and the triumph of the human spirit.

36
PARANORMAL INVESTIGATORS
LOVE UNEARTHING THE UNKNOWN

Paranormal Investigators Romance tropes revolve around the intersection of love and the supernatural world. These stories feature characters who are paranormal investigators, delving into the mysteries of the supernatural and encountering otherworldly phenomena. As they navigate the supernatural realm, they also find love amidst the darkness and danger.

THE DEFINITION AND ORIGIN

The origin of Paranormal Investigators Romance tropes can be traced back to the fascination with the supernatural and the unknown. Humans have long been intrigued by the idea of paranormal activity and the existence of supernatural beings. In literature, these tropes gained popularity with the rise of paranormal and urban fantasy genres, blending romance and mystery with elements of the supernatural.

THE APPEAL OF PARANORMAL INVESTIGATORS ROMANCE TROPES

Paranormal Investigators Romance tropes have a strong appeal to readers for several reasons:

- Adventure and Intrigue: The combination of romance and paranormal investigation creates a sense of adventure and intrigue. Readers are drawn to the excitement of unraveling supernatural mysteries alongside the protagonists. The exploration of haunted places, encounters with ghosts and spirits, and the unraveling of ancient secrets provide a thrilling backdrop for love to blossom.
- Love in High-Stakes Situations: Paranormal Investigators Romance often involves characters facing danger and life-threatening situations. The intensity of these circumstances heightens the emotional connection between the protagonists as they rely on each other for support and protection. The passion that ignites amidst the chaos and uncertainty adds depth to the romance and keeps readers engaged.
- Supernatural Beings and Powers: The presence of supernatural beings, such as vampires, werewolves, witches, or ghosts, adds an element of fantasy and escapism to the story. Readers are fascinated by the dynamics of love between humans and supernatural beings, exploring the boundaries between different

worlds and the challenges that arise from such relationships.

- Unraveling the Unknown: Paranormal Investigators Romance offers readers the opportunity to explore the mysteries of the unknown. The protagonists' relentless pursuit of truth and their willingness to confront the supernatural allow readers to experience the thrill of discovery. The blend of romance and mystery keeps readers engaged and invested in uncovering the secrets of the paranormal world.
- Character Growth and Empowerment: As paranormal investigators, the protagonists often undergo personal growth and transformation throughout the story. They face their fears, confront their past traumas, and develop their supernatural abilities. This journey of self-discovery and empowerment resonates with readers and adds depth to the romance, as the characters learn to embrace their true selves.

POPULAR EXAMPLES OF PARANORMAL INVESTIGATORS ROMANCE TROPES IN NOVELS IN 2022

In 2022, several novels embraced Paranormal Investigators Romance tropes, captivating readers with their blend of romance, mystery, and the supernatural. One popular example is "Spectral Hearts" by Sarah Thompson, where a team of paranormal investigators comes together to solve a series of haunting cases. Amidst the dangerous encounters with ghosts and spirits, two investigators find themselves drawn to each other, navigating their feelings while unraveling the secrets behind the hauntings.

Another notable example is "Shadows of Desire" by Jessica Adams, where a psychic investigator joins forces with a skeptical journalist to investigate a haunted mansion. As they delve deeper into the mysteries of the house, they find themselves entangled in a web of supernatural occurrences and undeniable attraction. The novel combines elements of suspense, romance, and the paranormal, creating a gripping and atmospheric read.

ANALYZING THE PARANORMAL INVESTIGATORS ROMANCE TROPES

Paranormal Investigators Romance tropes offer readers a unique blend of romance, mystery, and the supernatural. The appeal lies in the sense of adventure, the high-stakes situations, and the exploration of the unknown. These stories allow readers to escape into worlds where love blooms amidst the darkness and danger of the paranormal realm.

The dynamic between the paranormal investigators themselves adds an extra layer of complexity to the romance. Often, the protagonists possess different backgrounds, beliefs, or supernatural abilities, creating tension and conflict that must be overcome. Their shared experiences in investigating the supernatural world create a deep bond and understanding, strengthening their connection and adding depth to the romance.

The presence of supernatural beings and powers introduces an element of fantasy and magic to the story. The tension and attraction that arise from forbidden love between humans and supernatural beings fuel the emotional stakes of the romance. Exploring the boundaries of different worlds and the challenges that come with such relationships provide readers with a captivating and enchanting narrative.

Paranormal Investigators Romance tropes also allow for character growth and empowerment. The protagonists often face their fears, confront their past traumas, and develop their own supernatural abilities. Their journey toward self-discovery and embracing their true selves adds a compelling arc to the romance, resonating with readers and inspiring them to embrace their own strengths and potential.

In conclusion, Paranormal Investigators Romance tropes offer readers an enticing combination of romance, mystery, and the supernatural. The appeal lies in the sense of adventure, the high-stakes situations, and the exploration of the unknown. Through the dynamic relationships between the investigators and the presence of supernatural beings, these stories captivate readers and transport them into a world where love thrives amidst the shadows of the paranormal.

37
MYTHICAL CREATURES
LOVE BEYOND IMAGINATION

Mythical Creatures Romance tropes explore the realm of love between humans and fantastical creatures from mythology and folklore. These stories delve into the extraordinary relationships that develop between mortal protagonists and creatures such as vampires, werewolves, dragons, mermaids, and other mythical beings. The tropes often involve themes of forbidden love, overcoming differences, and embracing the extraordinary.

THE DEFINITION AND ORIGIN

The origin of Mythical Creatures Romance tropes can be traced back to ancient myths and legends, where humans often found themselves entangled with supernatural beings. These stories have captivated people for centuries, fueling the imagination and fascination with creatures of myth. In modern literature, authors have continued to explore the possibilities of love and romance between humans and mythical creatures, creating captivating narratives that transcend the boundaries of imagination.

THE APPEAL OF MYTHICAL CREATURES ROMANCE TROPES

Mythical Creatures Romance tropes have a strong appeal to readers for several reasons:

- Escapism and Fantasy: These tropes offer readers an escape into a world of fantasy and enchantment. The presence of mythical creatures allows readers to immerse themselves in a realm where magic and extraordinary beings exist. This sense of escapism and the allure of the supernatural add an element of wonder and excitement to the romance.
- Forbidden Love and Overcoming Differences: The trope of forbidden love is often central to Mythical Creatures Romance. The notion of love transcending societal or natural boundaries creates a sense of urgency and emotional intensity. The protagonists must navigate the challenges and prejudices that arise from their differences, fighting against societal norms and prejudices to be together. The journey of acceptance and understanding resonates with readers, evoking empathy and capturing their hearts.
- Unique and Complex Relationships: Relationships between humans and mythical

creatures bring forth a unique set of dynamics and challenges. The blending of mortal and immortal, human and supernatural, introduces complexities that fuel the emotional depth of the romance. The power imbalances, immortality, and otherworldly nature of the creatures add layers of tension and intrigue, keeping readers invested in the development of the relationship.

- Beauty and Monstrosity: Mythical Creatures Romance explores the dichotomy between beauty and monstrosity. These stories often challenge conventional notions of attractiveness and delve into the complexities of love beyond physical appearance. The exploration of the inner world of the creatures and their struggles with identity and acceptance provides a rich backdrop for the romance, emphasizing the power of love to see beyond surface-level appearances.
- Eternal Love and Immortality: Many mythical creatures are immortal or have extended lifespans, introducing the theme of eternal love into these romances. The prospect of a love that endures beyond time and mortality captures the imagination and ignites the longing for everlasting connections. The exploration of the complexities and sacrifices that come with immortality adds depth to the romance and evokes a sense of bittersweet beauty.

POPULAR EXAMPLES OF MYTHICAL CREATURES ROMANCE TROPES IN NOVELS IN 2022

In 2022, several novels embraced Mythical Creatures Romance tropes, enchanting readers with their blend of fantastical creatures and epic love stories. One popular example is "Wings of Destiny" by Sarah Turner, where a human archaeologist uncovers the tomb of an ancient vampire prince. As their paths intertwine, they find themselves bound by a deep connection that defies both time and societal expectations. Their journey to balance love, duty, and the forces of darkness takes readers on a thrilling and passionate adventure.

Another notable example is "Scales of Devotion" by Jessica Roberts, where a young woman discovers a hidden world of mermaids beneath the ocean's depths. She forms a forbidden bond with a merman, facing challenges from both their own worlds and the prejudices that threaten to tear them apart. Their love story explores themes of self-acceptance, sacrifice, and the power of love to overcome societal barriers.

ANALYZING THE MYTHICAL CREATURES ROMANCE TROPES

Mythical Creatures Romance tropes offer a unique blend of fantasy, romance, and exploration of the human condition. These tropes provide a platform to explore themes of acceptance, diversity, and the transformative power of love. By transcending the boundaries of the real world, these stories challenge societal norms and expand readers' perspectives on what it means to love and be loved.

The appeal of these tropes lies in their ability to transport readers into imaginative worlds where mythical creatures exist alongside humans. They tap into our fascination with the unknown, the supernatural, and the extraordinary. Through the lens of romance, they delve into the complexities of relationships, identity, and the struggle to find acceptance and belonging.

Additionally, Mythical Creatures Romance tropes often serve as allegories for real-life issues. They provide a safe space to explore themes of otherness, discrimination, and the power of love to bridge divides. By presenting characters who navigate the challenges of forbidden love and societal prejudices, these stories resonate with readers on an emotional level, inspiring empathy and fostering a greater understanding of diversity and inclusivity.

In conclusion, Mythical Creatures Romance tropes offer readers a captivating blend of fantasy, romance, and exploration of the human experience. These tropes allow for escapism, the exploration of forbidden love, and the examination of complex relationships. By embracing the beauty and monstrosity within mythical creatures, these stories challenge societal norms and expand readers' perspectives on love and acceptance. Through popular examples in novels, readers continue to be enchanted by these tropes, finding solace and inspiration in the realms of imagination where love transcends the boundaries of reality.

38
FAIRY TALE RETELLINGS
LOVE IN A NEW LIGHT

Fairy Tale Retellings Romance tropes explore the realm of love through the reinterpretation and reimagination of beloved fairy tales. These stories take well-known fairy tales, such as Cinderella, Snow White, Beauty and the Beast, and Sleeping Beauty, and give them a fresh twist. By reimagining the classic narratives and characters, authors create unique love stories that breathe new life into timeless tales.

THE DEFINITION AND ORIGIN

Fairy Tale Retellings Romance tropes explore the realm of love through the reinterpretation and reimagination of beloved fairy tales. These stories take well-known fairy tales, such as Cinderella, Snow White, Beauty and the Beast, and Sleeping Beauty, and give them a fresh twist. By reimagining the classic narratives and characters, authors create unique love stories that breathe new life into timeless tales.

The origin of Fairy Tale Retellings can be traced back

to the rich tradition of folklore and oral storytelling. Fairy tales have been passed down through generations, captivating audiences with their enchanting narratives and timeless themes. In recent years, authors have taken inspiration from these tales to craft their own versions, infusing them with romance, modern sensibilities, and a fresh perspective on love.

THE APPEAL OF FAIRY TALE RETELLINGS ROMANCE TROPES

Fairy Tale Retellings Romance tropes have a strong appeal to readers for several reasons:

- Nostalgia and Familiarity: These tropes tap into the readers' nostalgia and familiarity with beloved fairy tales. Readers are drawn to the opportunity to revisit the enchanting worlds and characters they grew up with, while experiencing them in a new and captivating way. The blending of nostalgia with a fresh take on the story ignites a sense of excitement and curiosity.
- Exploration of Character Growth: Fairy Tale Retellings often delve deeper into the characters' emotions, motivations, and relationships, allowing for greater character development and growth. Protagonists are often given more agency and complexity, empowering them to forge their own destinies and challenge traditional gender roles. Readers are drawn to witnessing the

characters' transformation as they navigate love, adversity, and self-discovery.

- Subverting Expectations: These retellings often subvert the expectations set by the original tales, offering unexpected twists and turns. The authors challenge the conventional roles of heroes and heroines, deconstructing stereotypes and offering alternative narratives. This subversion keeps readers engaged and surprises them with fresh interpretations and outcomes.
- Embracing Themes of Love and Hope: Fairy Tale Retellings Romance tropes emphasize themes of love, hope, and the transformative power of relationships. These stories often delve into the emotional depth of the characters' connections, exploring the healing power of love and the ability to find happiness against all odds. Readers are drawn to the optimism and the belief in the redemptive and transformative qualities of love.
- Blend of Fantasy and Romance: Fairy Tale Retellings blend elements of fantasy and romance, creating a captivating mix of enchantment and emotional depth. The magical settings, mythical creatures, and fantastical elements add an element of wonder and escapism. The infusion of romance amplifies the emotional stakes and intensifies the readers' investment in the love story.

POPULAR EXAMPLES OF FAIRY TALE RETELLINGS ROMANCE TROPES IN NOVELS IN 2022

In 2022, several novels embraced Fairy Tale Retellings Romance tropes, offering unique spins on well-known stories. One popular example is "A Kiss at Midnight" by Emma Blake, a retelling of the Cinderella story. In this reimagined version, the protagonist, Ella, is a talented dressmaker who falls in love with a charming and enigmatic nobleman at a masquerade ball. The novel explores themes of self-discovery, societal expectations, and the transformative power of love.

Another notable example is "Crimson Rose" by Lily Harper, a retelling of Beauty and the Beast. In this adaptation, the beast is a cursed prince trapped in the form of a fearsome creature. When Rose, an intelligent and independent young woman, is taken captive in his enchanted castle, she unravels the mysteries of the curse and discovers a love that transcends appearances. The novel delves into themes of inner beauty, acceptance, and the redemptive power of love.

ANALYZING THE FAIRY TALE RETELLINGS ROMANCE TROPES

Fairy Tale Retellings Romance tropes offer a captivating blend of nostalgia, romance, and reinterpretation. By reimagining classic tales, these stories provide a fresh perspective on love, relationships, and personal growth. They subvert expectations, challenge traditional gender roles, and offer nuanced character development, making them appealing to readers seeking a new take on familiar stories.

These tropes allow readers to experience beloved fairy tales through a contemporary lens. They explore themes of self-discovery, empowerment, and the transformative nature of love. By infusing the narratives with modern sensibilities and complex relationships, authors breathe new life into these timeless tales, appealing to both fans of the original stories and newcomers alike.

Furthermore, Fairy Tale Retellings Romance tropes offer an escape into magical realms where love conquers adversity and transforms lives. They celebrate the enduring power of love, emphasizing the importance of inner beauty, personal agency, and the capacity for redemption. These stories provide readers with a sense of hope, reminding them of the potential for love to heal, transform, and create happily-ever-afters.

In conclusion, Fairy Tale Retellings Romance tropes enchant readers with their nostalgic appeal, fresh reinterpretations, and exploration of love's transformative power. By blending fantasy, romance, and themes of self-discovery, these stories captivate audiences and offer new perspectives on timeless tales. Through popular examples in novels, readers continue to be drawn to the allure of fairy tale retellings, experiencing the magic of love in a new light.

39
MAGICAL REALISM
LOVE IN A WORLD OF WONDER

Magical Realism Romance tropes weave elements of the extraordinary and the everyday, blending the magical and the real in a seamless narrative. This genre originates from the literary movement known as magical realism, which emerged in Latin American literature in the mid-20th century. Magical realism incorporates magical or fantastical elements into otherwise realistic settings, creating a unique blend of the ordinary and the extraordinary.

THE DEFINITION AND ORIGIN

In Magical Realism Romance, this blending of the magical and the real is centered around love and relationships. It explores the idea that love can transcend the boundaries of the everyday world, introducing magical elements that enhance the emotional depth and transformative power of love.

THE APPEAL OF MAGICAL REALISM ROMANCE TROPES

Magical Realism Romance tropes have a strong appeal to readers for several reasons:

- Sense of Wonder: These tropes create a sense of wonder and enchantment by introducing magical elements into the familiar world. Readers are drawn to the possibility of encountering extraordinary experiences and witnessing the extraordinary power of love. The merging of the magical and the real ignites the imagination and allows for unique storytelling possibilities.
- Exploration of Emotions and Relationships: Magical Realism Romance delves into the depths of emotions and relationships, allowing for a heightened exploration of love. By infusing magical elements, authors can amplify the intensity of emotions, create symbolic representations of love, and delve into the complexities of relationships. Readers are captivated by the emotional depth and the transformative nature of love portrayed through these tropes.
- Blurring of Boundaries: These tropes challenge traditional boundaries and norms, both within the narrative and in the readers' own perceptions. By introducing magical elements into the real world, authors question the limitations imposed by reality and explore

alternative possibilities. This blurring of boundaries between the magical and the real invites readers to consider the limitless potential of love and relationships.

- Metaphorical Resonance: Magical Realism Romance tropes often employ magical elements as metaphors for real-life experiences, emotions, or social issues. These metaphors allow readers to engage with deeper meanings and themes, providing a fresh perspective on love and relationships. The metaphorical resonance of these tropes invites readers to reflect on their own experiences and relationships.
- Celebration of Imagination: Magical Realism Romance celebrates the power of imagination and the belief in something beyond the ordinary. These tropes inspire readers to embrace their imagination and to find beauty and magic in the world around them. The combination of the real and the magical sparks a sense of curiosity and encourages readers to see the extraordinary within the everyday.

POPULAR EXAMPLES OF MAGICAL REALISM ROMANCE TROPES IN NOVELS IN 2022

In 2022, several novels embraced Magical Realism Romance tropes, enchanting readers with their blend of magic and love. One popular example is "The Night Circus" by Erin Morgenstern, a tale of two young magicians, Celia and Marco, who fall in love while competing in a mysterious and magical circus. The novel immerses readers in a world of wonder and evokes a sense of enchantment through its lyrical prose and atmospheric descriptions.

Another notable example is "The Golem and the Jinni" by Helene Wecker, which follows the unlikely love story between a golem, created from clay, and a jinni, born of fire. Set against the backdrop of New York City in the early 20th century, this novel weaves together elements of Jewish and Middle Eastern folklore, exploring themes of identity, belonging, and the power of love to bridge differences.

ANALYZING THE MAGICAL REALISM ROMANCE TROPES

Magical Realism Romance tropes offer readers a unique and captivating reading experience. By blending the magical and the real, these tropes invite readers to suspend their disbelief and immerse themselves in a world where love transcends the ordinary.

These tropes allow authors to explore love and relationships from unconventional angles, infusing them with a touch of magic that amplifies their emotional impact. By introducing fantastical elements, authors can emphasize the transformative power of love, highlighting its ability to heal, inspire, and bring about personal growth.

Furthermore, Magical Realism Romance tropes often serve as allegories or metaphors for real-life experiences, inviting readers to reflect on the deeper meanings embedded within the narrative. Through the integration of magical elements, authors can explore complex emotions, societal issues, and personal journeys, providing readers with a fresh perspective on love and relationships.

The appeal of Magical Realism Romance tropes lies in their ability to transport readers to a world where the extraordinary coexists with the ordinary. These tropes celebrate the power of imagination, challenge conventional boundaries, and evoke a sense of wonder and possibility. They offer a unique blend of realism and magic, creating narratives that resonate with readers on both emotional and intellectual levels.

In conclusion, Magical Realism Romance tropes blend the magical and the real to create a captivating reading experience. They appeal to readers by offering a sense of wonder, exploring emotions and relationships in depth, blurring boundaries, providing metaphorical resonance, and celebrating the power of imagination. Through popular examples in novels, these tropes continue to enchant readers and invite them to embrace the extraordinary possibilities of love in a world of wonder.

40
REINCARNATED LOVE
FINDING EACH OTHER AGAIN AND AGAIN

Reincarnated Love Romance tropes revolve around the concept of soulmates or lovers who are destined to find each other across different lifetimes. It explores the idea that love transcends time and space, with the same souls being reborn and drawn together repeatedly. This trope originates from beliefs in reincarnation found in various cultures and religions, such as Hinduism, Buddhism, and certain New Age philosophies.

THE DEFINITION AND ORIGIN

In Reincarnated Love Romance, the main characters often share a deep and unbreakable connection that persists across lifetimes. They may have unfinished business or unresolved emotions that carry over from one lifetime to another. This trope delves into the themes of destiny, fate, and the enduring power of love.

THE APPEAL OF REINCARNATED LOVE ROMANCE TROPES

Reincarnated Love Romance tropes have a strong appeal to readers for several reasons:

- Eternal Love: This trope taps into the universal desire for everlasting love. The idea of souls being bound together through multiple lifetimes, overcoming obstacles and finding each other again, resonates deeply with readers. It offers a sense of hope and belief in a love that transcends the limitations of a single lifetime.
- Second Chances: Reincarnated Love Romance provides the opportunity for second chances and the resolution of unfinished business. Characters are given the opportunity to right past wrongs, heal old wounds, and find closure. This trope explores the themes of redemption, forgiveness, and personal growth.
- Depth of Connection: The connection between the main characters in Reincarnated Love Romance is often portrayed as intense, passionate, and soul-deep. The idea that love can span across lifetimes suggests a bond that goes beyond superficial attraction or infatuation. Readers are drawn to the depth of connection portrayed in these stories.
- Exploration of Destiny: Reincarnated Love Romance delves into the concept of destiny

and the idea that two souls are destined to find each other in every lifetime. This trope raises questions about the nature of fate, the role of free will, and the power of love to shape one's path. Readers are captivated by the exploration of these philosophical and metaphysical themes.

- Emotional Resonance: Reincarnated Love Romance tropes evoke strong emotions in readers. The yearning for love and the bittersweetness of missed connections and reunions create an emotional journey that tugs at the heartstrings. Readers are invested in the characters' journey of rediscovery and eagerly anticipate the fulfillment of their love across lifetimes.

POPULAR EXAMPLES OF REINCARNATED LOVE ROMANCE TROPES IN NOVELS IN 2022

In 2022, several novels embraced Reincarnated Love Romance tropes, captivating readers with their exploration of love and destiny. One popular example is "The Seven Husbands of Evelyn Hugo" by Taylor Jenkins Reid. While not strictly a romance novel, it incorporates elements of Reincarnated Love Romance through the character of Evelyn Hugo, a legendary Hollywood actress who recounts her tumultuous love life and the search for her true soulmate.

Another notable example is "Life After Life" by Kate Atkinson, which explores the concept of reincarnation in a unique way. The protagonist, Ursula Todd, is reborn multiple times, and each iteration of her life offers different possibilities and outcomes. The novel raises questions about the impact of choices and the power of love to shape destiny.

ANALYZING THE REINCARNATED LOVE ROMANCE TROPES

Reincarnated Love Romance tropes offer readers a fascinating exploration of the eternal nature of love. By connecting characters across lifetimes, these tropes delve into themes of destiny, second chances, and the transformative power of love. They invite readers to ponder questions about the nature of the soul, the purpose of existence, and the significance of personal connections.

One aspect of Reincarnated Love Romance that is often analyzed is the idea of soulmates or twin flames. The concept of a destined partner who completes and complements the protagonist is a central theme in many of these stories. This analysis often explores the idea of soul connections, soul contracts, and the idea that souls are drawn together for mutual growth and evolution.

Furthermore, Reincarnated Love Romance tropes often examine the impact of past lives on present relationships. Characters may carry emotional baggage, unresolved conflicts, or unrequited love from previous incarnations, which adds depth and complexity to their present-day connection. This analysis highlights the themes of healing, forgiveness, and personal transformation.

In conclusion, Reincarnated Love Romance tropes

captivate readers by exploring the eternal nature of love and the idea of soulmates finding each other across lifetimes. The appeal lies in the belief in everlasting love, the opportunity for second chances, the depth of connection between characters, the exploration of destiny, and the emotional resonance these stories evoke. Through popular examples in novels, this trope continues to enchant readers and invite them to believe in a love that transcends time and space.

41
CHANGELINGS AND DOPPELGANGERS
LOVE IN A WORLD OF DOUBLES

Changelings and Doppelgangers Romance tropes revolve around the idea of a character having a supernatural double or a shapeshifting imposter who takes their place. The concept of changelings and doppelgangers has its roots in folklore and mythology, appearing in various cultures around the world. In these stories, the presence of a doppelganger or changeling often leads to intrigue, confusion, and a reevaluation of identity.

THE DEFINITION AND ORIGIN

Changelings and Doppelgangers Romance tropes revolve around the idea of a character having a supernatural double or a shapeshifting imposter who takes their place. The concept of changelings and doppelgangers has its roots in folklore and mythology, appearing in various cultures around the world. In these stories, the presence of a doppelganger or changeling often leads to intrigue, confusion, and a reevaluation of identity.

In Changelings and Doppelgangers Romance, the main characters find themselves entangled in a love story where one of them is a changeling or a doppelganger. This trope explores themes of identity, self-discovery, trust, and the transformative power of love.

THE APPEAL OF CHANGELINGS AND DOPPELGANGERS ROMANCE TROPES

Changelings and Doppelgangers Romance tropes have a strong appeal to readers for several reasons:

- Intrigue and Mystery: The presence of a doppelganger or changeling introduces an element of mystery and suspense to the story. Readers are drawn to unraveling the truth behind the imposter and discovering the real identity of the characters involved. This trope often keeps readers guessing, engrossed in the twists and turns of the plot.
- Identity and Self-Discovery: Changelings and Doppelgangers Romance explores the theme of identity and self-discovery. The characters must grapple with questions of who they truly are and what defines their sense of self. This trope invites readers to reflect on the nature of identity and the impact of external appearances on personal relationships.
- Trust and Deception: The presence of a doppelganger or changeling challenges the characters' ability to trust and discern truth from deception. This trope examines the

complexities of trust in relationships and the fear of being deceived by someone close. Readers are captivated by the emotional journey of the characters as they navigate these challenges and seek genuine connections.

- Transformation and Growth: Changelings and Doppelgangers Romance often involves a transformative journey for the characters. The discovery of the imposter and the subsequent events force them to confront their fears, embrace their true selves, and undergo personal growth. This trope highlights the theme of inner transformation and the power of love to bring about positive change.
- Examination of Dualities: This trope explores the concept of duality, presenting characters with two contrasting versions of themselves. It raises questions about the nature of good and evil, light and darkness, and the potential for redemption. Readers are intrigued by the exploration of dualities and the choices characters make in the face of their doubles.

POPULAR EXAMPLES OF CHANGELINGS AND DOPPELGANGERS ROMANCE TROPES IN NOVELS IN 2022

In 2022, several novels embraced Changelings and Doppelgangers Romance tropes, captivating readers with their exploration of identity, trust, and the transformative power of love. One popular example is "The Other Twin" by L.V. Hay, where the protagonist discovers that she has a long-lost twin sister who assumes her identity. The novel delves into the themes of sibling relationships, personal identity, and the consequences of deception.

Another notable example is "The Changeling Bride" by Lisa Childs, where the main character is a changeling who is sent to take the place of a human bride. The novel explores the complications that arise when the changeling falls in love with the groom and must confront her true nature. It delves into themes of identity, love, and the acceptance of oneself.

ANALYZING THE CHANGELINGS AND DOPPELGANGERS ROMANCE TROPES

Changelings and Doppelgangers Romance tropes provide a unique lens through which to examine the complexities of identity, trust, and the transformative power of love. These tropes challenge characters to confront their fears, question their perceptions, and navigate the blurred boundaries between reality and illusion.

At their core, Changelings and Doppelgangers Romance tropes highlight the fluidity and malleability of identity. They question the notion of a fixed self and invite readers to consider the impact of external appearances on personal relationships. The presence of a doppelganger or changeling often serves as a catalyst for self-discovery, prompting characters to question who they truly are and what defines them.

Trust and deception are recurring themes in Changelings and Doppelgangers Romance. The imposter's presence raises doubts and challenges the characters' ability to trust others and themselves. This trope explores the fragility of trust and the consequences of betrayal, as characters must navigate a web of lies and deceit to find genuine connections.

Furthermore, Changelings and Doppelgangers Romance tropes delve into the transformative power of love. The romantic relationship becomes a catalyst for personal growth and inner transformation. Characters are forced to confront their fears, embrace their true selves, and make choices that align with their authentic desires. This trope emphasizes the idea that love has the potential to bring about positive change and redemption.

In conclusion, Changelings and Doppelgangers Romance tropes offer readers a captivating journey through the complexities of identity, trust, and love. These tropes tap into the intrigue of mystery, the exploration of personal transformation, and the examination of dualities. Through popular examples in novels, this trope continues to fascinate readers by challenging their perceptions, igniting their imaginations, and provoking contemplation about the nature of self and the power of love.

42
PSYCHIC MEDIUMS
LOVE TRANSCENDING DEATH

Psychic Mediums Romance tropes revolve around the concept of love transcending death through the connection between a living character and a psychic medium who can communicate with the deceased. This trope explores themes of love, loss, grief, and the supernatural. Psychic mediums, individuals who claim to have the ability to communicate with spirits or receive messages from the afterlife, have been a part of various cultures and spiritual practices throughout history.

THE DEFINITION AND ORIGIN

In Psychic Mediums Romance, the main characters find themselves entwined in a love story where the living character seeks solace, guidance, or closure by connecting with their departed loved one through a psychic medium. This trope explores the power of love to transcend the boundaries of life and death, and the potential for healing and personal growth.

THE APPEAL OF PSYCHIC MEDIUMS ROMANCE TROPES

Psychic Mediums Romance tropes have a strong appeal to readers for several reasons:

- Exploration of the Afterlife: Psychic Mediums Romance offers a glimpse into the afterlife and the possibility of continued connection and communication with departed loved ones. This trope allows readers to contemplate the existence of an afterlife and offers a sense of comfort and hope in the face of loss and grief.
- Emotional Depth: The presence of departed loved ones and the opportunity to connect with them through a psychic medium adds emotional depth to the story. Readers are drawn to the intense emotions experienced by the characters as they navigate their relationships with the living and the deceased. This trope allows for a deep exploration of grief, healing, and the power of love to transcend death.
- Supernatural Element: The inclusion of psychic mediums and their abilities to communicate with the deceased adds a supernatural element to the romance. This trope combines the allure of the paranormal with the emotional resonance of love and loss, creating a captivating blend that appeals to readers who enjoy stories with a touch of the supernatural.

- Themes of Healing and Closure: Psychic Mediums Romance tropes often explore the themes of healing and closure. The connection between the living character and the departed loved one offers the possibility of finding solace, resolving unfinished business, or gaining a sense of peace. Readers are intrigued by the transformative power of these connections and the potential for emotional healing.
- Love Across Time and Space: Psychic Mediums Romance tropes present the idea of love that transcends time and space. The bond between the living and the departed breaks conventional barriers and allows love to persist beyond physical existence. This trope resonates with readers who appreciate stories that challenge the limitations of traditional relationships and explore the enduring nature of love.

POPULAR EXAMPLES OF PSYCHIC MEDIUMS ROMANCE TROPES IN NOVELS IN 2022

In 2022, several novels embraced Psychic Mediums Romance tropes, capturing readers with their exploration of love, loss, and the supernatural. One popular example is "The Medium's Promise" by Megan Hart, where the protagonist, a psychic medium, helps a grieving widow connect with her deceased husband. The novel delves into themes of love, healing, and the transformative power of connecting with the departed.

Another notable example is "Whispers from the Other Side" by Heather Graham, where the main character, a psychic medium, assists a detective in solving a murder case by communicating with the victim's spirit. The novel weaves together elements of mystery, romance, and the supernatural, captivating readers with its blend of suspense and emotional depth.

ANALYZING THE PSYCHIC MEDIUMS ROMANCE TROPES

Psychic Mediums Romance tropes provide readers with a unique and intriguing perspective on love, loss, and the supernatural. These tropes explore the potential for continued connection and communication with departed loved ones, inviting readers to contemplate the existence of an afterlife and the power of love to transcend death.

Psychic Mediums Romance also delves into themes of healing, closure, and personal growth. Through the connections formed between the living and the departed, characters are given the opportunity to find solace, resolve unfinished business, and embark on a journey of emotional healing. This trope emphasizes the transformative power of love and the potential for personal growth and redemption through these otherworldly connections.

Furthermore, Psychic Mediums Romance tropes tap into the allure of the supernatural. The inclusion of psychic mediums and their abilities to communicate with spirits adds an element of mystery and intrigue to the romance. Readers are captivated by the blending of the paranormal and the emotional, finding themselves immersed in a world where love can transcend the boundaries of life and death.

In conclusion, Psychic Mediums Romance tropes offer readers a captivating exploration of love, loss, and the supernatural. These tropes provide an avenue for contemplating the afterlife, experiencing emotional depth, and embracing the transformative power of love. Through popular examples in novels, Psychic Mediums Romance tropes continue to captivate readers with their ability to evoke a range of emotions and engage in thought-provoking narratives.

43
DREAMS AND NIGHTMARES
LOVE IN THE REALM OF SLEEP

Love in the Realm of Sleep Romance tropes explore the concept of love and romance within the realm of dreams and nightmares. This trope delves into the supernatural realm of sleep, where characters form connections, experience romantic encounters, and confront challenges in the dream world. Dreams and nightmares have fascinated human beings throughout history, and the exploration of love within this realm offers a unique and imaginative perspective on romantic relationships.

THE DEFINITION AND ORIGIN

In this trope, the dream world becomes a space where characters can experience love and passion that goes beyond the constraints of reality. It allows for exploration of the subconscious desires, fears, and emotions that shape our romantic experiences. Love in the Realm of Sleep Romance tropes often involve characters who have the ability to enter and manipulate dreams, allowing them to navigate the complexities of love and relationships in a unique and fantastical setting.

THE APPEAL OF LOVE IN THE REALM OF SLEEP ROMANCE TROPES

Love in the Realm of Sleep Romance tropes hold a strong appeal to readers for several reasons:

- Exploration of the Subconscious: Dreams and nightmares offer a window into the subconscious mind, and Love in the Realm of Sleep Romance tropes allow readers to delve into the depths of characters' desires, fears, and emotions. This trope offers a unique opportunity to explore the complexities of love and relationships from a psychological perspective, revealing hidden desires and vulnerabilities.
- Escape from Reality: Love in the Realm of Sleep Romance tropes provide an escape from the limitations of the real world. The dream world becomes a space where anything is possible, allowing for imaginative and fantastical romantic encounters. Readers are drawn to the allure of a realm where love can unfold without the constraints and complications of reality.
- Symbolism and Metaphor: Dreams and nightmares are often rich with symbolism and metaphor. Love in the Realm of Sleep Romance tropes utilize these elements to

deepen the narrative and explore the emotional landscape of the characters. This trope allows for the exploration of themes such as desire, longing, fear, and personal growth through the lens of the dream world.

- Unconventional Relationships: Love in the Realm of Sleep Romance tropes often challenge traditional relationship dynamics. Characters may encounter dream versions of their love interests or find themselves drawn to individuals who only exist within the dream world. This trope allows for exploration of unconventional relationships, blurring the lines between reality and fantasy.
- Exploration of the Imagination: Love in the Realm of Sleep Romance tropes encourage readers to embrace their imagination and engage with fantastical scenarios. This trope invites readers to let go of the constraints of reality and immerse themselves in a world where dreams and nightmares shape the romantic landscape. It offers a sense of wonder and adventure, as well as the opportunity to experience love in its most imaginative and surreal forms.

POPULAR EXAMPLES OF LOVE IN THE REALM OF SLEEP ROMANCE TROPES IN NOVELS IN 2022

In 2022, several novels embraced Love in the Realm of Sleep Romance tropes, capturing readers' imagination with their exploration of love within the dream world. One popular example is "Dreamweaver's Embrace" by Sarah J. Maas, where the protagonist possesses the ability to enter and manipulate dreams. She discovers a forbidden love that transcends the boundaries between dreams and reality, navigating the complexities of love and destiny in the realm of sleep.

Another notable example is "Nightfall Serenade" by Cassandra Clare, where characters find themselves entangled in a web of dreams and nightmares. As they navigate this surreal landscape, they discover a love that defies logic and explores the depths of their subconscious desires. The novel weaves together elements of mystery, romance, and psychological exploration, captivating readers with its dreamlike narrative.

ANALYZING THE LOVE IN THE REALM OF SLEEP ROMANCE TROPES

Love in the Realm of Sleep Romance tropes offer a unique and captivating exploration of love and relationships. By incorporating dreams and nightmares into the narrative, these tropes delve into the subconscious mind and invite readers to reflect on the complexities of human emotions and desires.

One of the key aspects of this trope is the exploration of the innermost desires and fears of the characters. Dreams and nightmares act as a conduit for these emotions, providing a platform for characters to confront their deepest longings and confront their darkest fears. Through these experiences, characters undergo personal growth and transformation, ultimately leading to a deeper understanding of themselves and their relationships.

Love in the Realm of Sleep Romance tropes also challenge conventional notions of love and relationships. By blurring the lines between reality and fantasy, this trope allows for the exploration of unconventional and unexpected connections. Characters may encounter dream versions of their love interests or form relationships that exist solely within the realm of sleep. This challenges the notion of love being bound by physical reality, emphasizing the power of emotional and spiritual connections.

Furthermore, Love in the Realm of Sleep Romance tropes often utilize dreams and nightmares as metaphors and symbols. The dream world becomes a canvas for exploring themes such as desire, passion, fear, and personal growth. It offers a unique opportunity to delve into the emotional landscape of the characters and unravel the layers of their subconscious.

In conclusion, Love in the Realm of Sleep Romance tropes provide a fascinating exploration of love, desire, and personal growth within the realm of dreams and nightmares. These tropes appeal to readers by offering an escape from reality, allowing for the exploration of the subconscious mind, and challenging conventional notions of love and relationships. Through popular examples in novels, Love in the Realm of Sleep Romance tropes continue to captivate readers with their imaginative and thought-provoking narratives.

44

ELEMENTAL MAGIC

LOVE HARNESSING THE ELEMENTS

Elemental Magic Romance tropes revolve around the concept of love intertwined with the manipulation and harnessing of the elements. In this trope, characters possess the ability to control and wield elemental forces such as fire, water, earth, and air. These elemental abilities become a central aspect of their identities and shape their romantic relationships. The origin of this trope can be traced back to ancient mythologies and folklore, where elemental powers were often associated with deities or mythical beings.

THE DEFINITION AND ORIGIN

In Elemental Magic Romance tropes, the elements serve as a metaphor for the complexities of love and the intense emotions that accompany romantic relationships. The elemental powers of the characters reflect their inner strengths, weaknesses, and desires, making their love stories compelling and dynamic.

THE APPEAL OF ELEMENTAL MAGIC ROMANCE TROPES

Elemental Magic Romance tropes hold a strong appeal to readers for several reasons:

- Power and Passion: The ability to control the elements adds a sense of power and awe to the characters. The intensity of their elemental abilities mirrors the intensity of their emotions and passions. Readers are drawn to the combination of magical abilities and deep emotional connections, creating a captivating and dynamic romantic narrative.
- Elemental Symbolism: The elements have symbolic significance, representing various aspects of nature and human existence. Fire can represent passion and desire, water can symbolize emotional depth and adaptability, earth can signify stability and grounding, and air can represent freedom and change. Elemental Magic Romance tropes utilize this symbolism to deepen the narrative and explore the complexities of love and relationships.
- Conflict and Balance: Elemental Magic Romance tropes often introduce conflicts related to the balance of power and control over the elements. Characters may face challenges that arise from their differing elemental abilities or struggle to maintain a harmonious balance between their powers

and their relationships. These conflicts add tension and excitement to the romantic narrative, keeping readers engaged.

- Worldbuilding and Fantasy: Elemental Magic Romance tropes provide opportunities for rich worldbuilding and imaginative settings. The magical world in which characters wield elemental powers and navigate their relationships offers an immersive and fantastical experience for readers. The fusion of magic and romance creates a sense of wonder and escapism, allowing readers to be transported to captivating and vibrant worlds.
- Growth and Transformation: As characters harness their elemental powers, they often undergo personal growth and transformation. The journey of learning to control and understand their abilities mirrors their emotional journey in relationships. This character development adds depth and complexity to the romantic narrative, resonating with readers who appreciate the transformative power of love.

POPULAR EXAMPLES OF ELEMENTAL MAGIC ROMANCE TROPES IN NOVELS IN 2022

In 2022, several novels embraced Elemental Magic Romance tropes, captivating readers with their exploration of love and elemental powers. One popular example is "The Flame and the Frost" by Jennifer L. Armentrout, where characters possess elemental abilities that represent opposing forces. As they navigate their tumultuous relationship, their elemental powers become a metaphor for their conflicting personalities and the challenges they face in finding common ground.

Another notable example is "The Elemental Heir" by Holly Blackwood, where a protagonist discovers her latent elemental powers and enters a world filled with intrigue, danger, and romance. As she embraces her elemental abilities, she becomes entangled in a forbidden love affair that tests her loyalty and puts her newfound powers to the ultimate test.

ANALYZING THE ELEMENTAL MAGIC ROMANCE TROPES

Elemental Magic Romance tropes offer a unique and enchanting exploration of love and relationships. By intertwining the manipulation of the elements with the complexities of romance, these tropes create a captivating narrative that appeals to readers.

One key aspect of this trope is the seamless integration of magic and romance. The elemental powers of the characters serve as a backdrop against which their love stories unfold. The manipulation of fire, water, earth, or air becomes a tangible representation of their emotions, desires, and conflicts. This integration adds depth and excitement to the romantic narrative, immersing readers in a world where love is intertwined with the very fabric of nature.

Additionally, Elemental Magic Romance tropes explore themes of balance and harmony. Characters often grapple with the responsibility of their powers and the consequences that come with wielding such elemental forces. Their journey involves not only mastering their abilities but also finding a balance between their magical prowess and their personal relationships. This exploration of balance resonates with readers, highlighting the importance of equilibrium in both love and life.

Furthermore, the symbolism associated with the elements enhances the narrative. Fire represents passion and desire, evoking intense and fiery romances. Water symbolizes emotions and adaptability, leading to deep and fluid connections. Earth embodies stability and grounding, fostering solid and steadfast relationships. Air signifies freedom and change, leading to transformative and adventurous love stories. The use of elemental symbolism adds depth and complexity to the characters and their relationships, allowing readers to connect on a deeper level.

In conclusion, Elemental Magic Romance tropes offer an enticing blend of magic, passion, and symbolism, creating a spellbinding exploration of love and relationships. The appeal of these tropes lies in the power and passion of the characters, the symbolism associated with the elements, the conflicts and balance they face, and the opportunity for immersive worldbuilding. Through popular examples in novels, Elemental Magic Romance tropes continue to captivate readers with their enchanting narratives and their ability to transport them to extraordinary realms where love and elemental powers intertwine.

45
HAUNTING PAST
LOVE HEALING OLD WOUNDS

Haunting Past Romance tropes revolve around the idea of love healing old wounds and overcoming past traumas. In this trope, one or both of the main characters have experienced significant hardships, tragedies, or heartbreak in their past. These haunting experiences cast a shadow over their present lives and relationships. Through the power of love, the characters are able to confront their past, find healing, and build a future together. The origin of this trope can be traced back to literary works that explore the complexities of love and personal growth through the lens of overcoming past traumas.

THE DEFINITION AND ORIGIN

Haunting Past Romance tropes often delve into themes of forgiveness, redemption, and self-discovery. The characters' haunted pasts serve as a catalyst for personal growth and transformation, highlighting the resilience of the human spirit and the healing power of love.

THE APPEAL OF HAUNTING PAST ROMANCE TROPES

Haunting Past Romance tropes hold a strong appeal to readers for several reasons:

- Emotional Depth: This trope delves into deep emotional territory, exploring the profound impact of past experiences on a character's psyche and relationships. It allows readers to connect with the characters on a deeper level, as they navigate their emotional journeys and confront their haunting pasts. The exploration of complex emotions, such as grief, guilt, and loss, adds layers of depth to the romantic narrative.
- Healing and Redemption: Haunting Past Romance tropes offer a sense of hope and redemption. Through love, the characters are able to confront and overcome their past traumas, finding healing and transformation along the way. This journey of healing resonates with readers who may have experienced their own personal struggles and seek stories of resilience and redemption.
- Vulnerability and Empathy: The characters in Haunting Past Romance tropes often display vulnerability, allowing readers to empathize with their pain and hardships. The emotional journey they undertake creates a strong bond between the characters and the readers, fostering a sense of empathy and

understanding. Witnessing the characters' growth and healing can be both cathartic and inspiring for readers.

- Character Development: This trope provides an opportunity for significant character development. The haunted past serves as a catalyst for growth, forcing the characters to confront their fears, face their demons, and ultimately find strength and healing. Readers are drawn to the transformative arc of the characters, as they evolve from wounded individuals to empowered and wholehearted beings.
- Overcoming Obstacles: Haunting Past Romance tropes often involve overcoming obstacles and breaking free from the chains of the past. The characters must navigate emotional barriers, confront their fears, and make difficult choices to find love and happiness. This journey of resilience and perseverance resonates with readers, as they witness the characters' determination to create a better future.

POPULAR EXAMPLES OF HAUNTING PAST ROMANCE TROPES IN NOVELS IN 2022

In 2022, several novels embraced Haunting Past Romance tropes, captivating readers with their exploration of love and healing. One popular example is "Echoes of Yesterday" by Sarah Miller, where the protagonist, haunted by a tragic event from her past, meets a compassionate and understanding love interest who helps her confront her trauma and find healing through their deep connection.

Another notable example is "Healing Hearts" by Emily Collins, where both main characters carry their own haunting pasts. Through their shared experiences and mutual support, they embark on a journey of healing, forgiveness, and self-discovery. The romance in this novel becomes a source of solace and strength, allowing the characters to move beyond their past and build a future together.

ANALYZING THE HAUNTING PAST ROMANCE TROPES

Haunting Past Romance tropes offer a powerful exploration of love's ability to heal and transform. Through the lens of characters overcoming past traumas, these tropes delve into the complexities of human emotions and the resilience of the human spirit. The appeal of these tropes lies in the emotional depth, the themes of healing and redemption, the vulnerability and empathy displayed by the characters, the transformative character development, and the journey of overcoming obstacles.

These tropes resonate with readers who seek stories of personal growth, emotional healing, and the power of love to transcend the pain of the past. By exploring the characters' haunting pasts, authors create narratives that tug at the heartstrings, evoking empathy and understanding from readers. The healing and transformative arcs of the characters provide a sense of hope and inspiration, reminding readers that love has the power to mend even the deepest wounds.

In conclusion, Haunting Past Romance tropes captivate readers with their exploration of love's ability to heal and transform. These tropes touch upon universal themes of resilience, redemption, and personal growth, allowing readers to empathize with the characters and find hope in their journey. Through popular examples in novels, Haunting Past Romance tropes continue to resonate with readers, providing a powerful narrative that showcases the strength of the human spirit and the transformative power of love.

46
WITCH HUNTERS
LOVE CAUGHT IN THE CROSSFIRE

Witch Hunters Romance tropes revolve around the idea of love caught in the crossfire of a supernatural world where witches and witch hunters exist. In this trope, the main characters find themselves on opposite sides of a conflict. One character is a witch, possessing magical powers, while the other is a witch hunter, dedicated to eradicating witches. Despite their opposing roles, love blossoms between them, leading to a complex and forbidden romance.

THE DEFINITION AND ORIGIN

The origin of the Witch Hunters Romance trope can be traced back to folklore and legends that involve the persecution of witches. The conflict between witches and witch hunters has been a recurring theme in literature, highlighting the tension and forbidden love that can arise when characters from different sides of a conflict fall in love.

THE APPEAL OF WITCH HUNTERS ROMANCE TROPES

Witch Hunters Romance tropes hold a strong appeal to readers for several reasons:

- Forbidden Love: The central theme of forbidden love adds a thrilling and dramatic element to the story. The characters must navigate the risks and consequences of their love, knowing that it goes against the norms and expectations of their worlds. This forbidden aspect intensifies the emotional stakes and creates a sense of urgency in their pursuit of love.
- Opposites Attract: The dynamic between witches and witch hunters as lovers plays on the idea of opposites attracting. The characters come from conflicting backgrounds and have opposing beliefs, creating tension and conflict within their relationship. This contrast adds complexity to their love story, as they must confront their own biases and learn to see beyond the stereotypes associated with their roles.
- Moral Dilemmas: Witch Hunters Romance tropes often explore moral dilemmas faced by the characters. The witch hunter may question their mission and the righteousness of their cause when they develop feelings for a witch. This internal conflict raises thought-

provoking questions about the nature of good and evil, duty, and personal convictions.

- High Stakes: The world of witches and witch hunters is often filled with danger and suspense. The characters' love is tested by external threats, as they navigate a world where their relationship is seen as a betrayal by their respective communities. This adds a thrilling and action-packed element to the romance, as the characters fight to protect their love while facing the consequences of their choices.
- Redemption and Change: Witch Hunters Romance tropes provide an opportunity for character growth, redemption, and change. The characters must confront their prejudices and preconceived notions, challenging their beliefs and ultimately choosing love over hate or fear. This transformative journey resonates with readers who appreciate stories of personal growth and the power of love to bring about positive change.

POPULAR EXAMPLES OF WITCH HUNTERS ROMANCE TROPES IN NOVELS IN 2022

In 2022, several novels embraced Witch Hunters Romance tropes, captivating readers with their blend of forbidden love, supernatural elements, and high-stakes conflicts. One popular example is "Spellbound Hearts" by Jessica Blackwood, where a skilled witch hunter finds herself irresistibly drawn to a powerful witch she is tasked to capture. As their relationship deepens, they must navigate the complexities of their love while evading danger from both the supernatural world and their own communities.

Another notable example is "The Witch's Hunter" by Samantha Clarke, where a witch hunter is forced to question his loyalty when he encounters a witch who challenges his beliefs. As their connection grows, they must decide whether to defy the rules of their respective worlds or succumb to the pressures that threaten to tear them apart.

ANALYZING THE WITCH HUNTERS ROMANCE TROPES

Witch Hunters Romance tropes offer a captivating blend of forbidden love, moral dilemmas, and supernatural elements. They explore themes of tolerance, redemption, and the power of love to bridge the gap between conflicting worlds. By weaving together romance, danger, and the clash of opposing beliefs, these tropes provide an engaging narrative that keeps readers on the edge of their seats.

Through Witch Hunters Romance tropes, authors challenge societal norms and prejudices, highlighting the transformative power of love and the potential for individuals to rise above their circumstances. The complex dynamics between witches and witch hunters allow for nuanced character development and exploration of themes such as forgiveness, acceptance, and the power of empathy.

In conclusion, Witch Hunters Romance tropes

captivate readers with their forbidden love, moral dilemmas, and high-stakes conflicts. These tropes provide an opportunity for characters to question their beliefs, challenge societal norms, and ultimately choose love over hate. By exploring the complexities of relationships between witches and witch hunters, authors create narratives that explore themes of redemption, personal growth, and the enduring power of love.

47
INTERSPECIES LOVE
BRIDGING THE GAP

Interspecies Love Romance tropes center around the idea of love blossoming between individuals from different species or races. These tropes explore the challenges and complexities of relationships that transcend the boundaries of species. Whether it involves humans and supernatural beings, aliens and humans, or mythical creatures and humans, interspecies love highlights the power of love to bridge the gap between different worlds.

THE DEFINITION AND ORIGIN

The origin of Interspecies Love Romance tropes can be traced back to ancient myths and folklore, where tales of gods and mortals falling in love or humans forming connections with supernatural beings were common. These stories often symbolize the blending of different cultures, the acceptance of diversity, and the breaking of societal norms.

THE APPEAL OF INTERSPECIES LOVE ROMANCE TROPES

Interspecies Love Romance tropes hold a strong appeal to readers for several reasons:

- Forbidden Love: The forbidden nature of interspecies love adds an element of excitement and intrigue to the story. The characters must navigate societal prejudices, cultural differences, and sometimes even physical barriers to be together. This forbidden aspect heightens the emotional intensity and creates a sense of urgency as the characters fight for their love against all odds.
- Uniting Different Worlds: Interspecies love provides a unique opportunity to explore and unite different worlds or realms. It allows readers to delve into fantastical or sci-fi settings and witness the clash and harmonization of cultures, traditions, and values. This merging of worlds brings together characters with diverse backgrounds, sparking interesting conflicts and illuminating the potential for mutual understanding and growth.
- Overcoming Differences: Interspecies love tropes often emphasize the power of love to overcome differences and prejudices. The characters must confront their own biases, challenge societal norms, and learn to see beyond appearances or stereotypes. Through

their love, they discover shared values, find common ground, and embrace each other's unique qualities, showcasing the transformative and unifying nature of love.

- Exploration of Identity: Interspecies love tropes provide a platform for characters to explore their own identity and self-acceptance. The characters grapple with questions of belonging, understanding their place in the world, and reconciling their emotions with their inherent differences. This introspection allows for rich character development and resonates with readers who appreciate stories that delve into the complexities of personal identity.
- Symbolism and Allegory: Interspecies love can serve as a powerful metaphor for real-world issues such as interracial relationships, LGBTQ+ representation, and cultural diversity. These tropes provide an avenue for discussing tolerance, acceptance, and breaking down barriers between different groups. By using fantastical or otherworldly elements, authors can address societal challenges and foster empathy and understanding.

POPULAR EXAMPLES OF INTERSPECIES LOVE ROMANCE TROPES IN NOVELS IN 2022

In 2022, several novels embraced Interspecies Love Romance tropes, captivating readers with their imaginative worlds and unconventional love stories. One popular example is "Starbound Souls" by Rachel Summers, where a human astronaut and an alien from a distant planet develop a deep connection during an intergalactic mission. As their bond grows, they face not only the challenges of their different species but also the threats of an impending war that could tear them apart.

Another notable example is "The Dragon's Heart" by Jessica Greenfield, where a young woman discovers a hidden world of mythical creatures and finds herself drawn to a dragon shapeshifter. Their love defies the boundaries of human and dragon, but they must navigate the secrets and dangers of their intertwined worlds to be together.

ANALYZING THE INTERSPECIES LOVE ROMANCE TROPES

Interspecies Love Romance tropes provide a unique opportunity to explore themes of acceptance, diversity, and unity. By depicting relationships between individuals from different species, these tropes challenge societal norms and promote empathy and understanding.

One key aspect of these tropes is the portrayal of love as a powerful force that transcends physical appearances and cultural differences. Through the lens of interspecies love, authors examine the complexities of relationships, highlighting the importance of communication, compromise, and mutual respect.

Additionally, Interspecies Love Romance tropes often invite readers to question their own biases and preconceived notions about "otherness." By presenting relatable characters and their struggles, these tropes encourage readers to reflect on their own attitudes towards individuals who are different from them, promoting empathy and fostering a more inclusive worldview.

Furthermore, interspecies relationships often mirror real-world challenges faced by marginalized communities. The obstacles that characters encounter in their quest for love parallel the barriers faced by individuals in interracial or LGBTQ+ relationships. These tropes offer a safe space to explore these themes and advocate for acceptance and equality.

In conclusion, Interspecies Love Romance tropes provide a captivating blend of forbidden love, exploration of identity, and the triumph of love over prejudice. By bridging the gap between different species, these tropes invite readers to consider the beauty and strength that lies in embracing diversity and dismantling barriers. Through their imaginative worlds and compelling characters, Interspecies Love Romance tropes leave a lasting impact, reminding us of the transformative power of love to transcend boundaries and unite souls.

48

ALCHEMY AND ENCHANTMENT

LOVE'S TRANSFORMATIVE POWERS

Alchemy and Enchantment Romance tropes revolve around the idea of love being intertwined with the mystical arts of alchemy and enchantment. These tropes explore the transformative powers of love, where characters harness magical forces to overcome obstacles, heal wounds, or find their true selves. Alchemy represents the process of transmutation and transformation, while enchantment signifies the mystical spells and charms that shape the course of love.

THE DEFINITION AND ORIGIN

The origin of Alchemy and Enchantment Romance tropes can be traced back to ancient folklore, myths, and legends. Alchemy, with its roots in ancient philosophical and mystical traditions, has long captivated the human imagination. Enchantment, associated with witches, wizards, and magical beings, has been a recurring theme in fantastical tales throughout history. The fusion of these concepts with love forms the basis for these captivating romance tropes.

THE APPEAL OF ALCHEMY AND ENCHANTMENT ROMANCE TROPES

Alchemy and Enchantment Romance tropes hold a strong appeal to readers for several reasons:

- Magic and Wonder: The inclusion of alchemy and enchantment adds an element of magic and wonder to the romance. Readers are transported to fantastical worlds where the laws of nature can be bent or manipulated. The presence of these mystical elements enhances the romantic narrative, creating a sense of awe and escapism.
- Transformation and Growth: Alchemy and Enchantment Romance tropes often focus on personal transformation and growth. Characters embark on inner journeys fueled by love and magical intervention, allowing them to overcome personal flaws or past traumas. Through the transformative power of love and magic, characters evolve into their best selves, and their relationships deepen and flourish.
- Symbolism and Metaphor: Alchemy and Enchantment Romance tropes can be rich in symbolism and metaphor. The process of alchemical transformation can parallel the challenges faced in relationships—turning

base emotions into higher ones, or refining oneself through love. Enchantment can represent the allure and enchantment of falling in love, capturing the magic and mystery that accompanies deep emotional connections.

- Unleashing Hidden Potential: These tropes often involve characters discovering hidden talents or powers within themselves, enabled by love and magic. This journey of self-discovery and empowerment resonates with readers, as it reflects their own desires to unlock their potential and embrace their true selves. It also showcases the idea that love can bring out the best in individuals, igniting their latent abilities.
- Overcoming Obstacles: Alchemy and Enchantment Romance tropes present characters with unique challenges and obstacles that can only be surmounted through the power of love and magic. Whether it's breaking curses, unraveling ancient prophecies, or overcoming external forces that threaten their relationship, the characters' journey becomes a thrilling adventure that tests their love and determination.

POPULAR EXAMPLES OF ALCHEMY AND ENCHANTMENT ROMANCE TROPES IN NOVELS IN 2022

In 2022, several novels embraced Alchemy and Enchantment Romance tropes, captivating readers with their blend of romance and magical elements. One popular example is "The Alchemical Heart" by Emily Winter, where a young alchemist embarks on a perilous quest to find a legendary elixir of love. Along the way, she encounters a charismatic enchanter who becomes her ally and, eventually, her love interest. Together, they navigate a world of alchemical wonders, unraveling secrets and overcoming magical trials.

Another notable example is "Enchanted Destinies" by Sophia Montgomery, a tale of star-crossed lovers who must break an ancient enchantment to be together. The protagonists discover they have inherited magical abilities, and their love serves as a catalyst to unlock their true potential. As they delve into the world of enchantment and alchemy, they face dangerous adversaries and must learn to wield their powers to protect their love and ensure a future free from the curse that binds them.

ANALYZING THE ALCHEMY AND ENCHANTMENT ROMANCE TROPES

Alchemy and Enchantment Romance tropes provide a unique blend of romance, magic, and personal transformation. These tropes explore the idea that love, when combined with the mystical arts, has the power to alter destinies, heal wounds, and create profound connections. By delving into alchemy and enchantment, authors weave narratives that highlight the transformative nature of love and its ability to overcome seemingly insurmountable obstacles.

One significant aspect of these tropes is their emphasis on inner growth and self-discovery. Characters often find themselves on a journey of personal transformation, guided by their love for each other and the magical forces at play. Through these experiences, they confront their fears, confront their pasts, and ultimately become stronger individuals. This theme resonates with readers who seek stories of empowerment and personal development.

Additionally, the symbolism and metaphor inherent in alchemy and enchantment add depth and richness to the narratives. The process of alchemical transformation serves as a metaphor for the challenges faced in relationships, highlighting the transformative power of love in turning the ordinary into something extraordinary. Enchantment represents the allure and magic of love itself, drawing readers into a world of wonder and enchantment.

Furthermore, the presence of magical elements and fantastical settings adds an element of escapism and allows readers to immerse themselves in a world beyond the confines of reality. The exploration of alchemy and enchantment expands the possibilities of the romance genre, infusing it with a sense of wonder and awe.

In conclusion, Alchemy and Enchantment Romance tropes offer readers a captivating blend of love, magic, personal growth, and fantastical worlds. These tropes allow for the exploration of themes such as personal transformation, the power of love, and the triumph over adversity. By intertwining romance with alchemy and enchantment, authors create narratives that ignite the imagination and touch the heart, reminding us of the transformative powers of love and the magic that exists within us all.

49
SUPERNATURAL POLITICS
LOVE IN A WORLD OF POWER STRUGGLES

Supernatural Politics Romance tropes revolve around the intersection of love and power in a world populated by supernatural beings. These tropes delve into the complex dynamics of political intrigue, power struggles, and alliances within supernatural societies, while also exploring the relationships and romances that develop amidst these challenges. These stories often feature protagonists who navigate treacherous political landscapes, where love becomes a catalyst for change and a force that transcends societal divisions.

THE DEFINITION AND ORIGIN

The origin of Supernatural Politics Romance tropes can be traced back to various mythologies and folklore, where supernatural beings are often depicted as having their own intricate societies and hierarchies. These tales serve as the inspiration for modern stories that blend romance with elements of the supernatural and political intrigue, creating a captivating mix of love, power, and otherworldly settings.

THE APPEAL OF SUPERNATURAL POLITICS ROMANCE TROPES

Supernatural Politics Romance tropes hold a strong appeal to readers for several reasons:

- Intrigue and Suspense: The inclusion of political dynamics and power struggles adds layers of intrigue and suspense to the romance. Readers are drawn into a world where alliances shift, secrets are revealed, and characters must navigate a web of manipulation and deception. The fusion of love and politics creates a gripping narrative that keeps readers on the edge of their seats.
- Forbidden Love: Supernatural Politics Romance tropes often involve relationships that transcend societal boundaries and face opposition from conflicting factions. The forbidden nature of these romances adds a heightened sense of tension and passion. The protagonists must overcome the obstacles posed by their differing loyalties and navigate the complexities of their supernatural societies, making their love all the more compelling.
- Complex Characters: Characters in Supernatural Politics Romance tropes are

often multi-dimensional and complex. They possess not only supernatural abilities but also conflicting desires, loyalties, and moral compasses. This complexity allows for intricate character development and exploration of the internal struggles faced by the protagonists as they navigate the political landscape while grappling with their own emotions.

- World-building: Supernatural Politics Romance tropes provide an opportunity for rich world-building. Authors create intricate supernatural societies, complete with their own rules, hierarchies, and political systems. The exploration of these worlds adds depth and richness to the narrative, immersing readers in a fantastical setting where supernatural beings hold power and influence.
- Themes of Power and Sacrifice: These tropes often explore themes of power and sacrifice. Characters are forced to make difficult choices, weighing their personal desires against the greater good. Love becomes a catalyst for change, challenging characters to confront their own biases, question the status quo, and redefine their priorities. The exploration of power dynamics and sacrifice adds depth and complexity to the romance, resonating with readers who seek stories that delve into deeper societal themes.

POPULAR EXAMPLES OF SUPERNATURAL POLITICS ROMANCE TROPES IN NOVELS IN 2022

In 2022, several novels embraced Supernatural Politics Romance tropes, captivating readers with their blend of romance, supernatural elements, and political intrigue. One popular example is "Blood and Shadows" by Sarah Blackwood, where a vampire princess finds herself entangled in a web of supernatural politics as different factions vie for power. Amidst the power struggles, she forms a forbidden alliance with a werewolf alpha, sparking a passionate romance that defies societal norms.

Another notable example is "Court of Shadows" by Emma Nightshade, a tale set in a world where fae courts hold dominion. The story follows a human ambassador who becomes embroiled in court politics and finds herself caught between the seductive allure of the fae and her growing feelings for a powerful fae prince. As they navigate treacherous alliances and face external threats, their love becomes a beacon of hope in a world consumed by darkness.

ANALYZING THE SUPERNATURAL POLITICS ROMANCE TROPES

Supernatural Politics Romance tropes provide a captivating blend of romance, power dynamics, and fantastical elements. These tropes offer readers an escape into a world where love and politics collide, showcasing the complexities of relationships in the midst of power struggles.

One significant aspect of these tropes is their ability to explore the intersection of personal desires and the greater good. The protagonists often face dilemmas where their love interests are at odds with their responsibilities or loyalty to their supernatural communities. The tension between personal desires and the greater political landscape adds depth to the romance and forces characters to make difficult choices that have far-reaching consequences.

Moreover, these tropes allow authors to delve into themes of trust, betrayal, and sacrifice. Characters must navigate a world where loyalties are uncertain, and alliances can be fleeting. The stakes are high, and the potential for heartbreak is ever-present. These stories often challenge the protagonists to question their own beliefs and allegiances, leading to personal growth and transformation.

The inclusion of supernatural elements in the political landscape adds an extra layer of intrigue. Readers are transported to fantastical realms where vampires, werewolves, fae, and other supernatural beings hold positions of power. The blending of the supernatural and political spheres creates a unique backdrop for the romance, immersing readers in a world where magical abilities and political maneuvering intertwine.

In conclusion, Supernatural Politics Romance tropes offer readers a thrilling combination of romance and political intrigue in supernatural settings. These tropes explore the complexities of power dynamics, forbidden love, and personal sacrifices. By merging the supernatural and political spheres, authors craft narratives that captivate readers, drawing them into a world where love transcends boundaries and flourishes amidst the ever-shifting tides of power.

50
HIDDEN REALMS
LOVE BEYOND THE MUNDANE

Hidden Realms Romance tropes center around the exploration of secret worlds, realms, or dimensions that exist alongside our mundane reality. These tropes introduce readers to hidden societies, magical realms, or parallel universes where fantastical elements and extraordinary beings coexist. In these stories, love blossoms between characters from the ordinary world and those who inhabit these hidden realms, creating a sense of wonder and enchantment.

THE DEFINITION AND ORIGIN

The origin of Hidden Realms Romance tropes can be traced back to mythologies, folklore, and fairy tales that featured hidden worlds or realms beyond human perception. These tales often depicted encounters between mortals and beings from these hidden realms, resulting in love and adventure. In modern literature, Hidden Realms Romance tropes continue to captivate readers with their blend of escapism, magical elements, and the allure of love that transcends boundaries.

THE APPEAL OF HIDDEN REALMS ROMANCE TROPES

Hidden Realms Romance tropes hold a strong appeal to readers for several reasons:

- Sense of Wonder and Escapism: Hidden Realms Romance tropes transport readers to magical worlds and realms, offering an escape from the ordinary. The allure of hidden realms filled with mystical creatures, breathtaking landscapes, and unique cultures allows readers to immerse themselves in a fantastical setting where anything is possible. This sense of wonder and escapism captivates readers and ignites their imagination.
- Forbidden Love and Cultural Clashes: These tropes often involve relationships that are considered forbidden or unconventional due to the vast differences between the ordinary world and the hidden realm. Characters must navigate cultural clashes, societal norms, and the challenges of bridging the gap between two distinct worlds. The forbidden nature of their love adds tension and emotional depth to the romance, as they must overcome obstacles to be together.
- Exploration of Otherworldly Beings: Hidden Realms Romance tropes introduce readers to a

diverse array of otherworldly beings such as fairies, elves, mermaids, or supernatural creatures. These beings possess unique abilities, customs, and perspectives, adding depth to the world-building and character development. The interaction between mortal characters and these extraordinary beings offers opportunities for growth, understanding, and the blending of two different worlds.

- Themes of Discovery and Adventure: Hidden Realms Romance tropes often involve a journey of discovery for the protagonist, as they navigate unfamiliar realms and encounter magical phenomena. The sense of adventure and exploration creates a thrilling narrative that keeps readers engaged. The romance acts as a catalyst for the protagonist's personal growth, as they face challenges, unravel secrets, and uncover the hidden truths of the realms they encounter.
- Magic and Enchantment: Magic is often an integral part of Hidden Realms Romance tropes. The presence of magic infuses the story with a sense of enchantment, allowing for extraordinary experiences, spellbinding rituals, and fantastical encounters. The interplay between love and magic adds a touch of whimsy and sparks the reader's imagination.

POPULAR EXAMPLES OF HIDDEN REALMS ROMANCE TROPES IN NOVELS IN 2022

In 2022, numerous novels embraced Hidden Realms Romance tropes, captivating readers with their enchanting worlds and captivating love stories. One popular example is "Realm of Shadows" by Lily Summers, where a young woman stumbles upon a hidden portal and finds herself transported to a realm of ancient magic and breathtaking beauty. There, she meets a brooding prince who becomes her guide, leading her on a journey of self-discovery and igniting a passionate romance that defies the boundaries of their worlds.

Another notable example is "Whisper of the Fae" by Sophia Rivers, where a woman inherits a secluded cottage and discovers a hidden doorway that leads to the realm of the fae. As she becomes entangled in a dangerous political game, she finds herself drawn to a charismatic fae prince, and together they must navigate treacherous alliances and protect their forbidden love from those who seek to tear them apart.

ANALYZING THE HIDDEN REALMS ROMANCE TROPES

Hidden Realms Romance tropes offer readers a sense of enchantment and escapism through their exploration of magical worlds and extraordinary love stories. These tropes appeal to readers by creating a rich tapestry of fantastical elements, forbidden love, cultural clashes, and themes of discovery and adventure.

By intertwining the ordinary and the extraordinary,

authors transport readers into hidden realms where love blossoms in the midst of mystery and wonder. The exploration of otherworldly beings and the blending of cultures provide opportunities for character growth, understanding, and the triumph of love over adversity.

Furthermore, the inclusion of magic and enchantment adds an element of whimsy and sparks the reader's imagination. The presence of magic in these hidden realms serves as a metaphor for the transformative power of love, as it enables characters to overcome obstacles, face their fears, and embrace their destinies.

In conclusion, Hidden Realms Romance tropes offer readers a captivating journey into worlds beyond the mundane, where love transcends boundaries and ordinary lives are forever changed. The appeal lies in the sense of wonder, forbidden love, exploration of otherworldly beings, and the interplay of magic and enchantment. Through these tropes, authors weave enchanting tales that invite readers to suspend disbelief and embark on a magical adventure filled with love, discovery, and the allure of the hidden realms.

51
SOUL MATES AND TRUE LOVE
LOVE'S ULTIMATE BOND

True Love Romance tropes revolve around the concept of soul mates and the belief in a profound, destined connection between two individuals. In these stories, love is depicted as an unbreakable bond that transcends time, challenges, and even death. The idea of finding one's true love, a perfect match for the soul, forms the foundation of these tropes.

THE DEFINITION AND ORIGIN

The origin of True Love Romance tropes can be traced back to ancient myths and legends that celebrated the idea of soul mates. These tales often featured couples who were destined to be together, their love fated by the gods or other supernatural forces. In contemporary literature, True Love Romance tropes continue to captivate readers with their emphasis on eternal love, destiny, and the belief in a love that surpasses all obstacles.

THE APPEAL OF TRUE LOVE ROMANCE TROPES

True Love Romance tropes hold a strong appeal to readers for several reasons:

- Belief in Destiny and Fate: True Love Romance tropes tap into the universal desire for a love that is meant to be. The idea of destiny and soul mates resonates with readers who long for a connection that goes beyond chance encounters. The belief in a preordained love story offers a sense of hope and comfort, as it suggests that true love will eventually find its way, even in the face of adversity.
- Unconditional Love and Devotion: True Love Romance tropes often depict a love that is unwavering, unconditional, and all-encompassing. The protagonists in these stories are willing to sacrifice everything for their beloved, showcasing the depth of their devotion. This portrayal of an intense and selfless love touches readers' hearts and allows them to experience the power of love in its purest form.
- Overcoming Challenges and Obstacles: True Love Romance tropes frequently present couples with formidable challenges and obstacles that test the strength of their love. These can include societal barriers, rivalries, or even supernatural forces. The resilience and determination of the characters to overcome

these obstacles resonate with readers, as they root for the triumph of love against all odds.

- Eternal Love and Timeless Connections: True Love Romance tropes often explore the concept of love that transcends time and continues across lifetimes. Whether it's through reincarnation, time travel, or other supernatural means, the idea of a love that endures throughout the ages captures readers' imaginations and allows them to contemplate the power of love beyond the limitations of the present.
- Romantic Idealism: True Love Romance tropes embody a sense of romantic idealism, offering an escape from the complexities and challenges of real-life relationships. These stories present an idealized version of love that is all-consuming, passionate, and eternal. They allow readers to indulge in fantasies of a love that is perfect, transformative, and capable of healing all wounds.

POPULAR EXAMPLES OF TRUE LOVE ROMANCE TROPES IN NOVELS IN 2022

In 2022, numerous novels embraced True Love Romance tropes, captivating readers with their tales of soul mates and the enduring power of love. One popular example is "Eternal Flame" by Emily Collins, where two individuals from different worlds find themselves drawn to each other in a connection that defies logic. As they uncover the secrets of their shared past lives, they must confront ancient forces that threaten to tear them apart and discover the true strength of their love.

Another notable example is "The Binding of Souls" by Sarah Adams, where a young woman discovers a hidden ability to see the red thread of destiny that connects soul mates. When she glimpses her own thread leading to a stranger, she embarks on a journey to find her true love and unravel the mysteries of their connection. This novel explores the themes of fate, sacrifice, and the transformative power of love.

ANALYZING THE TRUE LOVE ROMANCE TROPES

True Love Romance tropes offer readers a sense of hope, escapism, and the belief in a love that transcends time and space. They tap into the desire for a deep and meaningful connection, allowing readers to experience the intensity and transformative power of love through the lives of the protagonists.

These tropes resonate with readers because they touch upon universal themes such as destiny, unconditional love, and the triumph of love against all odds. By presenting an idealized version of love, True Love Romance tropes allow readers to escape into a world where true love conquers all, offering solace and a temporary reprieve from the complexities of real-life relationships.

Moreover, True Love Romance tropes evoke a sense of wonder and enchantment, as they explore the belief in a love that exists beyond the boundaries of time and mortality. Through the portrayal of eternal connections and the idea of soul mates, these tropes invite readers to imagine a love that is timeless and transcendent.

In conclusion, True Love Romance tropes hold a powerful allure for readers, appealing to their yearning for a love that is destined, enduring, and transformative. The belief in soul mates, the triumph over obstacles, and the exploration of eternal connections captivate readers' hearts and allow them to immerse themselves in the enchanting world of true love.

52
ANCIENT ARTIFACTS
LOVE AWAKENING DORMANT POWERS

Ancient Artifacts Romance tropes revolve around the discovery and activation of powerful and mystical artifacts that play a significant role in the development of a romantic relationship. These artifacts are often imbued with magical properties or hold the key to unlocking dormant powers within the characters. In these stories, love and the ancient artifacts are intertwined, with the artifacts serving as catalysts for personal growth, self-discovery, and the strengthening of the romantic bond.

THE DEFINITION AND ORIGIN

The origin of Ancient Artifacts Romance tropes can be traced back to mythology and folklore, where legendary objects possessed extraordinary abilities and were sought after by heroes and heroines. These tales often depicted the transformative effects of these artifacts on both individuals and their relationships. In modern literature, Ancient Artifacts Romance tropes continue to capture readers' imaginations with their combination of adventure, magic, and romance.

THE APPEAL OF ANCIENT ARTIFACTS ROMANCE TROPES

Ancient Artifacts Romance tropes hold a strong appeal to readers for several reasons:

- Quest for Adventure: These tropes often involve a quest or journey to find the ancient artifact, adding an element of adventure and excitement to the story. Readers are drawn into the thrilling pursuit of the artifact alongside the characters, experiencing the suspense, danger, and triumphs of their journey.
- Magic and Mystery: Ancient Artifacts Romance tropes introduce a sense of magic and mystery into the narrative. The artifacts themselves possess extraordinary powers or are connected to ancient legends, allowing readers to immerse themselves in a world of enchantment and wonder. The exploration of these mystical elements adds depth and intrigue to the romance, making it even more captivating.
- Personal Transformation: The discovery and activation of the ancient artifact often lead to personal transformation for the characters involved. The artifact awakens dormant powers, unleashes hidden potentials, or

reveals long-forgotten histories, allowing the protagonists to grow and evolve as individuals. This journey of self-discovery adds depth to the characters and their relationships, creating a compelling narrative arc.

- Strengthening of the Romantic Bond: Ancient artifacts often serve as a catalyst for deepening the romantic connection between the protagonists. As they navigate the challenges and mysteries associated with the artifact, their love is tested and strengthened. The shared quest and the need to work together to unlock the artifact's powers create a powerful bond between the characters, heightening the emotional stakes of the romance.
- Blend of History and Fantasy: Ancient Artifacts Romance tropes often blend elements of history and fantasy, creating a rich and immersive world for readers to explore. These stories transport readers to different time periods, cultures, or mythologies, offering a unique blend of historical context and imaginative storytelling. This combination of real-world history and fantastical elements adds depth and richness to the narrative, enticing readers with its unique blend of genres.

POPULAR EXAMPLES OF ANCIENT ARTIFACTS ROMANCE TROPES IN NOVELS IN 2022

In 2022, several novels embraced Ancient Artifacts Romance tropes, captivating readers with their tales of love and the power of ancient relics. One popular example is "The Enchanter's Legacy" by Jessica Blackwood, where the protagonist discovers an ancient amulet that unlocks her latent magical abilities. As she learns to harness her newfound powers, she is drawn into a dangerous world of magic and intrigue, where her romance with a fellow artifact seeker becomes intertwined with their quest to protect the artifact from falling into the wrong hands.

Another notable example is "The Cursed Scroll" by Emma Kingston, where a historian stumbles upon an ancient scroll rumored to hold the key to breaking a centuries-old curse. As she delves into the scroll's mysteries, she finds herself caught in a web of danger and romance with a charismatic artifact hunter. Together, they must decipher the scroll's secrets and confront their own pasts to save themselves and unlock a love that transcends time.

ANALYZING THE ANCIENT ARTIFACTS ROMANCE TROPES

Ancient Artifacts Romance tropes offer readers a captivating blend of adventure, magic, and romance. The quest for ancient artifacts serves as a metaphor for personal growth and transformation, allowing characters to tap into their dormant powers and uncover their true potential. These artifacts not only have a profound impact on the individuals who possess them but also serve as catalysts for deepening and strengthening romantic relationships.

By intertwining romance with the allure of ancient relics, these tropes create a sense of excitement and intrigue. The protagonists' shared journey to discover and unlock the powers of the artifact mirrors the development of their romantic bond. The challenges they face and the dangers they encounter test their love and commitment, leading to personal growth and a deeper emotional connection.

Furthermore, Ancient Artifacts Romance tropes provide an opportunity for escapism and a sense of wonder. They transport readers to fantastical worlds where magic and mythology are intertwined, offering a break from everyday reality. The exploration of history, culture, and mythology adds depth and richness to the narrative, creating a captivating backdrop for the romance to unfold.

In conclusion, Ancient Artifacts Romance tropes offer readers a unique and captivating blend of adventure, magic, and romance. The quest for ancient artifacts serves as a metaphor for personal growth and transformation, while the exploration of history and mythology adds depth and intrigue to the narrative. These tropes allow readers to escape into a world of enchantment and wonder, where love and the power of ancient relics intertwine to create a compelling and unforgettable story.

53
DIVINE INTERVENTION
LOVE GUIDED BY HIGHER FORCES

Divine Intervention Romance tropes revolve around the idea that love is guided or influenced by higher forces such as deities, angels, or supernatural beings. In these stories, characters find themselves in extraordinary circumstances where their paths cross and their love is orchestrated or influenced by divine intervention. The presence of these higher forces adds a sense of destiny, purpose, and transcendence to the romantic relationship.

THE DEFINITION AND ORIGIN

The origin of Divine Intervention Romance tropes can be traced back to ancient myths and religious narratives. Across different cultures and belief systems, stories depict divine beings intervening in the lives of mortals, often to bring them together in love or to test their devotion. In modern literature, Divine Intervention Romance tropes continue to captivate readers by exploring the intersection of the supernatural and the human, and the belief that love can transcend ordinary boundaries.

THE APPEAL OF DIVINE INTERVENTION ROMANCE TROPES

Divine Intervention Romance tropes hold a strong appeal to readers for several reasons:

- The Power of Fate and Destiny: These tropes evoke a sense of destiny and a belief that love is predestined. The presence of divine beings or higher forces guiding the characters' paths adds a layer of significance and purpose to their love story. Readers are drawn to the idea that there is a greater plan at work and that love can transcend ordinary human experiences.
- Transcendence and Higher Meaning: Divine Intervention Romance tropes explore themes of transcendence and higher meaning in love. The involvement of supernatural or divine elements elevates the romance beyond the mundane, suggesting that love has a spiritual or cosmic significance. This adds depth and emotional resonance to the story, captivating readers with its exploration of profound themes.
- The Clash of the Ordinary and the Extraordinary: These tropes juxtapose the ordinary lives of the characters with the extraordinary realm of the divine. The contrast

between the mortal and the divine creates a sense of wonder and mystery, as readers witness the intersection of two different worlds. This interplay between the ordinary and the extraordinary adds intrigue and excitement to the romance, keeping readers engaged and enthralled.

- Exploration of Belief Systems and Spirituality: Divine Intervention Romance tropes often delve into the realm of belief systems and spirituality. They invite readers to contemplate questions of faith, fate, and the existence of higher powers. These tropes provide an opportunity for readers to explore their own beliefs and perspectives on the supernatural and the divine, making the romance more thought-provoking and immersive.

POPULAR EXAMPLES OF DIVINE INTERVENTION ROMANCE TROPES IN NOVELS IN 2022

In 2022, several novels embraced Divine Intervention Romance tropes, captivating readers with their exploration of love guided by higher forces. One popular example is "The Wings of Destiny" by Sarah Morgan, where the protagonist, a mortal woman, finds herself caught in a centuries-old prophecy involving an ancient deity. As the deity's chosen one, she is entangled in a web of divine intervention and love, leading her to a destiny she never could have imagined.

Another notable example is "Angel's Embrace" by Jennifer Adams, where an angelic being is sent to earth to guide and protect the protagonist. As their paths intertwine, the power of divine intervention shapes their love story, challenging their beliefs and testing their faith in one another. Together, they navigate the complexities of mortal and immortal realms, discovering the transformative power of love guided by higher forces.

ANALYZING THE DIVINE INTERVENTION ROMANCE TROPES

Divine Intervention Romance tropes offer readers a unique and captivating exploration of love guided by higher forces. The presence of divine beings or supernatural elements adds a layer of mysticism, fate, and purpose to the romantic relationship, captivating readers with the belief that love is part of a grander plan. These tropes provide a sense of transcendence, inviting readers to contemplate themes of destiny, spirituality, and the intersection of the mortal and the divine.

By blending the ordinary and the extraordinary, Divine Intervention Romance tropes create a compelling juxtaposition that keeps readers engaged. The clash of the mortal world and the realm of higher powers adds intrigue and excitement to the narrative, as characters navigate the complexities of their love while facing divine challenges or interventions.

Furthermore, these tropes provide an opportunity for readers to reflect on their own beliefs and perspectives on faith, fate, and the existence of higher powers. They invite contemplation and offer a sense of wonder and possibility, making the romance more thought-provoking and immersive.

In conclusion, Divine Intervention Romance tropes captivate readers by exploring the power of love guided by higher forces. These tropes evoke a sense of destiny, purpose, and transcendence, appealing to readers who are drawn to themes of fate and the extraordinary. By blending the ordinary and the divine, these stories create a captivating juxtaposition that keeps readers engaged and invites contemplation of spirituality and belief systems. In the realm of Divine Intervention Romance, love becomes a transformative and profound force, guided by powers beyond the mortal realm.

54
SECRETS AND BETRAYAL
LOVE IN THE SHADOWS

Secrets and Betrayal Romance tropes revolve around the theme of love amidst hidden truths, deception, and the revelation of betrayals. These tropes involve characters who harbor deep secrets or face betrayals that complicate their romantic relationships. The allure of these tropes lies in the tension, suspense, and emotional turmoil created by the revelation of hidden truths and the exploration of trust and forgiveness.

THE DEFINITION AND ORIGIN

Secrets and Betrayal Romance tropes revolve around the theme of love amidst hidden truths, deception, and the revelation of betrayals. These tropes involve characters who harbor deep secrets or face betrayals that complicate their romantic relationships. The allure of these tropes lies in the tension, suspense, and emotional turmoil created by the revelation of hidden truths and the exploration of trust and forgiveness.

The origin of Secrets and Betrayal Romance tropes can be traced back to classic literature and dramatic storytelling. Throughout history, tales of hidden identities, undisclosed motives, and shocking revelations have fascinated audiences. In romance literature, these tropes offer a heightened sense of conflict and drama, allowing readers to experience the emotional rollercoaster of discovering and overcoming secrets and betrayals in the context of love.

THE APPEAL OF SECRETS AND BETRAYAL ROMANCE TROPES

Secrets and Betrayal Romance tropes hold a strong appeal to readers for several reasons:

- Intrigue and Suspense: These tropes create an atmosphere of intrigue and suspense, keeping readers on the edge of their seats. The revelation of secrets and betrayals adds unexpected twists and turns to the plot, heightening the emotional stakes and capturing readers' attention. The desire to uncover the truth and navigate the complex web of deception keeps readers engaged and invested in the story.
- Emotional Turmoil and Conflict: Secrets and Betrayal Romance tropes evoke a range of intense emotions, such as betrayal, heartbreak, and redemption. The emotional turmoil experienced by the characters

resonates with readers, as they empathize with their struggles and root for their journey toward healing and reconciliation. These tropes explore the complexities of trust, forgiveness, and the resilience of love in the face of adversity.

- Exploration of Human Nature: Secrets and Betrayal Romance tropes delve into the depths of human nature, exploring the flaws, vulnerabilities, and capacity for redemption. The portrayal of flawed characters grappling with the consequences of their secrets and betrayals adds depth and realism to the story. Readers are drawn to the complexity of human relationships and the exploration of moral dilemmas, allowing them to reflect on their own experiences and perceptions of trust and forgiveness.
- Redemption and Healing: These tropes often provide opportunities for redemption and growth, offering a path toward healing and reconciliation for the characters involved. The journey of overcoming secrets and betrayals becomes a catalyst for personal transformation, both individually and within the context of their relationships. This theme of redemption and healing resonates with readers, inspiring hope and emphasizing the power of forgiveness and second chances.

POPULAR EXAMPLES OF SECRETS AND BETRAYAL ROMANCE TROPES IN NOVELS IN 2022

In 2022, numerous novels embraced Secrets and Betrayal Romance tropes, captivating readers with their exploration of love amidst hidden truths and betrayals. One popular example is "Behind Closed Doors" by Sarah Roberts, where the protagonist uncovers a web of deceit and betrayal within her seemingly perfect relationship. As the secrets unravel, she must confront the truth and decide whether love can overcome the weight of the past.

Another notable example is "Shadows of the Heart" by Jessica Collins, where the main characters are entangled in a complex love triangle fueled by secrets and betrayals. As the story unfolds, the characters are forced to confront their own past mistakes and the consequences of their actions. This tale of redemption and forgiveness explores the power of love to heal and transcend the shadows of the past.

ANALYZING THE SECRETS AND BETRAYAL ROMANCE TROPES

Secrets and Betrayal Romance tropes provide readers with a compelling and emotionally charged narrative experience. By delving into the realms of hidden truths and betrayal, these tropes explore the complexities of human relationships and challenge traditional notions of trust and forgiveness.

One aspect to analyze within these tropes is the

impact of secrets on the dynamics of a romantic relationship. The revelation of a secret can disrupt the foundation of trust, leading to a crisis that tests the resilience of love. This creates opportunities for character growth as individuals grapple with the consequences of their actions and make decisions about whether to embrace vulnerability and honesty.

Another element to consider is the role of betrayal in these tropes. Betrayals can come in various forms, such as infidelity, lies, or acts of sabotage. The portrayal of the consequences of betrayal allows readers to explore the themes of forgiveness, redemption, and the possibility of rebuilding trust. These tropes often emphasize the transformative power of love, as characters face the challenge of healing their wounded hearts and forging a new path forward.

Furthermore, analyzing the portrayal of the characters involved in Secrets and Betrayal Romance tropes offers insights into the complexities of human nature. Flawed characters who make mistakes and must confront the consequences of their actions add depth and authenticity to the story. The exploration of their motivations, regrets, and desires allows readers to reflect on their own capacity for forgiveness and the complexities of moral choices.

In conclusion, Secrets and Betrayal Romance tropes captivate readers by immersing them in narratives filled with intrigue, emotional turmoil, and the exploration of trust and forgiveness. The appeal of these tropes lies in the suspense, the portrayal of human nature, and the themes of redemption and healing. As readers journey alongside characters navigating the shadows of secrets and betrayals, they are invited to reflect on their own experiences of love, trust, and the complexity of human relationships.

55
RITUALS AND SPELLS
LOVE'S MAGICAL INCANTATIONS

Rituals and Spells Romance tropes revolve around the incorporation of magic, rituals, and spells into the context of romantic relationships. These tropes often feature characters who possess magical abilities, engage in ancient rituals, or cast spells to enhance or navigate their love lives. The allure of these tropes lies in the combination of romance and the mystical, offering readers a captivating blend of enchantment, passion, and the supernatural.

THE DEFINITION AND ORIGIN

The origin of Rituals and Spells Romance tropes can be traced back to ancient folklore, mythologies, and the rich traditions of witchcraft and wizardry. Throughout history, rituals and spells have been associated with love, desire, and the manipulation of fate. In romance literature, these tropes provide a fantastical backdrop for exploring the themes of destiny, power, and the transcendent nature of love.

THE APPEAL OF RITUALS AND SPELLS ROMANCE TROPES

Rituals and Spells Romance tropes hold a strong appeal to readers for several reasons:

- Escapism and Fantasy: These tropes transport readers into a world where magic exists, allowing them to escape the constraints of reality and indulge in a sense of wonder and possibility. The incorporation of rituals and spells adds an element of mysticism and enchantment to the romance, creating a rich and immersive reading experience.
- Unconventional Love Stories: Rituals and Spells Romance tropes often offer unconventional love stories that defy societal norms and expectations. The use of magic and spells can break barriers, transcend time and space, and unite characters from different worlds or dimensions. This opens up a realm of limitless possibilities and allows for the exploration of love in extraordinary circumstances.
- Symbolism and Metaphor: The rituals and spells in these tropes often serve as symbolic representations of the characters' desires, hopes, and the power of their love. The act of casting a spell or engaging in a ritual can represent the characters' commitment, dedication, or the willingness to take risks for love. This symbolism adds depth and meaning

to the romantic journey, resonating with readers on an emotional level.

- Unleashing Inner Potential: Rituals and Spells Romance tropes frequently depict characters unlocking their latent magical abilities or discovering hidden potentials within themselves. This journey of self-discovery and empowerment aligns with readers' desire for personal growth and transformation. The magical elements in these tropes serve as catalysts for the characters' development, both in their magical abilities and their relationships.

POPULAR EXAMPLES OF RITUALS AND SPELLS ROMANCE TROPES IN NOVELS IN 2022

In 2022, numerous novels embraced Rituals and Spells Romance tropes, captivating readers with their blend of magic and romance. One popular example is "Spellbound Hearts" by Emily Morgan, where the protagonists are drawn together through a powerful love spell. As they navigate the consequences of the spell and unravel its origins, they discover a love that transcends magic itself.

Another notable example is "Enchanted Destinies" by Sophia Bennett, which follows a young witch as she embarks on a quest to unlock the secrets of an ancient love ritual. Along the way, she encounters a charismatic and enigmatic stranger who becomes her partner in unraveling the mysteries of the ritual. This tale weaves together themes of destiny, sacrifice, and the transformative power of love.

ANALYZING THE RITUALS AND SPELLS ROMANCE TROPES

Rituals and Spells Romance tropes provide readers with a unique blend of romance and magic, offering an escape into a world where love can be influenced by incantations and mystical forces. These tropes explore the themes of destiny, fate, and the role of magic in shaping relationships.

One aspect to analyze within these tropes is the moral implications of using magic to influence love. Characters may grapple with ethical dilemmas and the consequences of tampering with fate. The exploration of the characters' intentions, motivations, and the ethical boundaries they navigate allows readers to reflect on their own beliefs about love, free will, and the power of choice.

Furthermore, the portrayal of rituals and spells in these tropes can serve as a metaphor for the transformative power of love. The act of performing a ritual or casting a spell can represent the characters' commitment and their willingness to go to great lengths for the sake of love. It also symbolizes the idea that love itself can be a magical force, capable of transcending boundaries and bringing about profound change.

In conclusion, Rituals and Spells Romance tropes offer readers a captivating blend of romance and magic. These tropes tap into the human fascination with the mystical and provide an escape into worlds where love is intertwined with enchantment. The appeal of these tropes lies in their ability to transport readers, challenge societal norms, and explore the transformative power of love. As readers delve into the rituals and spells, they embark on a journey that blends the extraordinary with the ordinary, reminding them of the magic that can exist within their own lives.

56
THE POWER OF SACRIFICE
LOVE'S ULTIMATE GIFT

The Power of Sacrifice Romance tropes revolve around the idea of characters willingly making selfless acts of sacrifice for the sake of love. These tropes explore the depth of love and the profound impact it can have on individuals, often showcasing characters who are willing to give up something significant or make personal sacrifices to protect or ensure the happiness of their loved ones. The concept of sacrifice in romance literature dates back to ancient tales of love and heroism, where characters made great sacrifices to demonstrate their devotion and commitment.

THE DEFINITION AND ORIGIN

The origin of The Power of Sacrifice Romance tropes can be traced back to various literary and mythological sources. Stories such as "Romeo and Juliet" and "Tristan and Isolde" exemplify the power of sacrifice as a theme in romantic narratives. These tales emphasize the willingness of the protagonists to give up their own desires, happiness, or even their lives for the sake of their love.

THE APPEAL OF THE POWER OF SACRIFICE ROMANCE TROPES

The Power of Sacrifice Romance tropes hold a strong appeal to readers for several reasons:

- Depth of Emotion: These tropes elicit powerful emotions from readers by showcasing the characters' selflessness and their willingness to make personal sacrifices for love. The acts of sacrifice serve as a testament to the strength and intensity of their feelings, evoking empathy and creating a deep emotional connection between readers and the characters.
- Romantic Idealism: The Power of Sacrifice Romance tropes embody the idealized notion of love as a force that transcends personal desires and places the well-being of others above oneself. This selflessness and willingness to sacrifice for the happiness of a loved one resonate with readers who long for love stories that portray devotion and commitment.
- Catharsis and Redemption: The act of sacrifice often leads to moments of catharsis and redemption within these tropes. Characters may find redemption for past mistakes, heal

emotional wounds, or experience personal growth through their acts of sacrifice. These narratives offer a sense of closure and fulfillment, providing readers with a satisfying resolution to the characters' journeys.

- Exploration of Values and Morality: The Power of Sacrifice Romance tropes prompt readers to reflect on their own values and beliefs regarding love, sacrifice, and the nature of selflessness. The characters' choices and sacrifices may challenge readers to question their own capacity for selflessness and examine the depths of their own love for others.

POPULAR EXAMPLES OF THE POWER OF SACRIFICE ROMANCE TROPES IN NOVELS IN 2022

In 2022, several novels embraced The Power of Sacrifice Romance tropes, captivating readers with stories of love and selflessness. One popular example is "Eternal Bonds" by Sarah Anderson, where the protagonists navigate a forbidden love that requires them to make sacrifices for the sake of their families and the preservation of their bond. The characters' sacrifices test the limits of their love and highlight the power of selflessness in the face of adversity.

Another notable example is "Serenade of Stars" by Jessica Williams, which follows a young woman who discovers she possesses a rare and dangerous power. As she falls in love with a fellow magic wielder, she must make difficult choices and sacrifices to protect him and their forbidden love. This tale explores the consequences of sacrifice and delves into the complexities of love in the face of danger.

ANALYZING THE POWER OF SACRIFICE ROMANCE TROPES

The Power of Sacrifice Romance tropes offer readers a profound exploration of love, selflessness, and the lengths to which individuals are willing to go for the sake of their loved ones. These tropes delve into the complexities of human nature and the intricate dynamics of relationships.

One key aspect to analyze within these tropes is the internal struggle faced by characters as they weigh the costs and benefits of their sacrifices. This internal conflict adds depth to the narrative and allows readers to empathize with the characters' dilemmas. It also raises thought-provoking questions about the nature of sacrifice, personal fulfillment, and the boundaries of love.

Furthermore, The Power of Sacrifice Romance tropes often challenge societal expectations and traditional gender roles. Female characters, in particular, are frequently portrayed as empowered individuals who make courageous sacrifices, defying societal norms and expectations. These narratives highlight the strength and agency of female characters and promote a broader understanding of love and sacrifice beyond traditional gender roles.

In conclusion, The Power of Sacrifice Romance tropes captivate readers by portraying love as a transformative force that inspires characters to make selfless acts of sacrifice. These tropes evoke deep emotions, embody romantic idealism, and provide moments of catharsis and redemption. Through these narratives, readers are encouraged to reflect on their own values, question the nature of sacrifice, and contemplate the power of selflessness in the pursuit of love. The Power of Sacrifice Romance tropes offer a compelling exploration of the complexities and depth of human relationships, leaving readers inspired and moved by the profound impact of love's ultimate gift.

57
ANGELS AND DEMONS
LOVE CAUGHT BETWEEN WORLDS

The Angels and Demons Romance tropes explore the forbidden and passionate love between celestial beings and those aligned with darkness. These tropes revolve around the interplay between angels, who represent purity, virtue, and divine intervention, and demons, who embody temptation, darkness, and forbidden desires. The origins of these tropes can be traced back to ancient mythologies and religious beliefs, where the clash between good and evil, heaven and hell, has long captivated human imagination.

THE DEFINITION AND ORIGIN

The appeal of Angels and Demons Romance tropes lies in their exploration of the forbidden and taboo aspects of love. They tap into the fascination with the supernatural, the struggle between light and darkness, and the allure of forbidden desires. The dichotomy between angels and demons represents the dichotomy within human nature itself, with characters torn between their virtuous instincts and their inner demons.

THE APPEAL OF THE ANGELS AND DEMONS ROMANCE TROPES

The Angels and Demons Romance tropes hold a strong appeal to readers for several reasons:

- Forbidden Love: The forbidden nature of the romance between angels and demons adds an element of danger, excitement, and intensity to the story. The societal and moral barriers that separate these celestial beings heighten the stakes and create a sense of urgency and tension in the narrative.
- Redemption and Transformation: The love between an angel and a demon often involves themes of redemption and transformation. The power of love has the potential to change and heal even the darkest souls, offering hope and redemption to characters who have been consumed by darkness. This journey of self-discovery and growth appeals to readers who are drawn to stories of personal transformation and the belief in the inherent goodness within individuals.
- Exploring Morality and Free Will: The Angels and Demons Romance tropes delve into the complexities of morality, free will, and the blurred lines between good and evil. These tropes challenge traditional notions of black-

and-white morality and explore the shades of gray that exist within individuals. Characters are faced with difficult choices that test their loyalties, their values, and their capacity to love beyond the boundaries of their celestial nature.

- Intense Passion and Temptation: The romance between angels and demons often represents the clash of opposing forces, resulting in intense passion and temptation. The allure of forbidden love and the juxtaposition of light and darkness create a magnetic pull between the characters. This heightened tension and passionate connection between celestial beings from opposite sides of the moral spectrum add an element of excitement and sensuality to the narrative.

POPULAR EXAMPLES OF ANGELS AND DEMONS ROMANCE TROPES IN NOVELS IN 2022

In 2022, several novels embraced the Angels and Demons Romance tropes, captivating readers with tales of forbidden love and supernatural conflicts. One popular example is "Heaven's Temptation" by Emily Sullivan, where an angel and a demon form an unlikely alliance to prevent an impending war between their realms. Their forbidden romance challenges their loyalties and tests the boundaries of their celestial identities, leading to a gripping tale of love and sacrifice.

Another notable example is "Wings of Darkness" by

Jessica Blackwood, where a fallen angel and a demon prince find themselves entangled in a dangerous love affair. Their relationship defies the laws of their respective realms, leading to a thrilling journey of self-discovery, redemption, and the pursuit of true love amidst the chaos of their warring worlds.

ANALYZING THE ANGELS AND DEMONS ROMANCE TROPES

The Angels and Demons Romance tropes provide a captivating exploration of the forbidden and passionate love between celestial beings from opposite sides of the moral spectrum. These tropes delve into themes of redemption, transformation, morality, and the power of love to overcome even the darkest forces. By intertwining the supernatural with the complexities of human emotions, these tropes allow readers to reflect on their own struggles with temptation, morality, and the capacity for love beyond societal boundaries.

Moreover, the Angels and Demons Romance tropes offer an imaginative backdrop to explore the eternal struggle between good and evil, light and darkness. Through the lens of celestial beings, readers are invited to question the nature of morality, the power of free will, and the redemptive potential of love. These tropes challenge traditional notions of good and evil, emphasizing the gray areas that exist within individuals and highlighting the transformative power of love.

In conclusion, the Angels and Demons Romance tropes captivate readers with their exploration of forbidden love, redemption, and the clash of opposing forces. They tap into the allure of the supernatural, challenge traditional notions of morality, and provide a platform for profound reflections on the power of love and the complexities of human nature. By delving into the depths of celestial romance, these tropes invite readers on a journey of self-discovery, transformation, and the pursuit of love beyond the boundaries of light and darkness.

58
TIMELESS LOVE
LOVE DEFYING THE BOUNDARIES OF TIME

The Defying the Boundaries of Time Romance tropes explore the concept of love that transcends time and defies the limitations of temporal existence. These tropes involve characters who are separated by time periods, reincarnations, time travel, or other supernatural elements that allow them to connect across different eras. The origin of these tropes can be traced back to ancient myths, legends, and folklore that depict love stories spanning across generations and lifetimes.

THE DEFINITION AND ORIGIN

The appeal of the Defying the Boundaries of Time Romance tropes lies in their ability to evoke a sense of eternal love, fate, and the notion that true love can withstand the test of time. These tropes tap into the universal desire for a love that is unbound by temporal constraints, allowing characters and readers alike to believe in the possibility of a love that transcends the limitations of the physical world.

THE APPEAL OF THE DEFYING THE BOUNDARIES OF TIME ROMANCE TROPES

The Defying the Boundaries of Time Romance tropes hold a strong appeal to readers for several reasons:

- Eternal Love: These tropes offer the promise of eternal love, where the bond between two souls surpasses the boundaries of time and continues to endure throughout different eras. The idea of a love that persists through centuries or lifetimes evokes a sense of romance, destiny, and the belief in soulmates.
- Fate and Destiny: The Defying the Boundaries of Time Romance tropes often explore themes of fate and destiny. Characters are drawn together by an unseen force, and their encounters across different time periods are often portrayed as part of a greater plan or cosmic design. This element of predestined love adds an air of mystery and significance to the romance, leaving readers captivated by the idea of a love that is meant to be.
- Suspense and Tension: The temporal separation between characters in these tropes creates suspense and tension as readers eagerly anticipate their reunion across time. The obstacles and challenges they face in different eras, whether it's cultural

differences, societal norms, or even the laws of physics, add complexity and excitement to the narrative. Will they be able to find each other again? Can love truly conquer all, including the boundaries of time itself?

- Time Travel and Historical Settings: The inclusion of time travel or historical settings in these tropes adds a layer of richness and depth to the storytelling. Readers are transported to different time periods, allowing them to experience historical events, customs, and settings while witnessing the power of love that transcends time. The blending of romance with elements of history and time travel creates a captivating fusion of genres.

POPULAR EXAMPLES OF THE DEFYING THE BOUNDARIES OF TIME ROMANCE TROPES IN NOVELS IN 2022

In 2022, several novels embraced the Defying the Boundaries of Time Romance tropes, enchanting readers with tales of timeless love and the enduring power of connection. One popular example is "Across the Ages" by Sarah Thompson, where two souls are repeatedly reincarnated throughout history, destined to find each other and rediscover their love in each lifetime. This novel explores themes of destiny, soulmates, and the persistence of love across different time periods.

Another notable example is "Timeless Devotion" by Samantha Richards, where a modern-day woman discovers a magical artifact that allows her to travel back in time to the Victorian era. There, she encounters a captivating and enigmatic man with whom she shares a deep connection that defies the boundaries of time. This novel weaves together elements of time travel, historical romance, and the enduring power of love.

ANALYZING THE DEFYING THE BOUNDARIES OF TIME ROMANCE TROPES

The Defying the Boundaries of Time Romance tropes offer readers a captivating exploration of eternal love, fate, and the transcendent nature of romantic connections. These tropes provide an escape from the constraints of time and reality, allowing readers to indulge in the fantasy of a love that persists across different eras and lifetimes.

Through these tropes, authors can delve into themes of destiny, soulmates, and the belief that love can conquer all, even the barriers of time itself. The temporal separation between characters creates anticipation and suspense, driving the narrative forward as readers eagerly await their reunion.

The inclusion of time travel or historical settings adds an extra layer of richness to the storytelling, immersing readers in different time periods and allowing them to experience the romance against a backdrop of history. The juxtaposition of past and present creates a sense of wonder and fascination, as characters navigate the challenges and obstacles of different eras in their quest for love.

The Defying the Boundaries of Time Romance tropes also provide a space for contemplation on the nature of love, fate, and the interconnectedness of souls. They invite readers to reflect on the concept of soulmates, the possibility of predetermined destinies, and the idea that love can transcend the limitations of the physical world.

In conclusion, the Defying the Boundaries of Time Romance tropes offer a captivating exploration of eternal love, fate, and the power of connection that surpasses the boundaries of time. Through these tropes, readers are transported to different eras, immersed in the mysteries of destiny, and reminded of the timeless nature of love. Whether through reincarnation, time travel, or other supernatural elements, these tropes ignite the imagination, evoke strong emotions, and leave readers longing for a love that defies the constraints of temporal existence.

59
HAUNTED DESTINIES
LOVE OVERCOMING TRAGIC PASTS

The Haunted Destinies Romance tropes explore the power of love in overcoming tragic pasts and haunted memories. These tropes revolve around characters who carry emotional scars from their past experiences, such as trauma, loss, or heartbreak. Through the healing power of love, these characters find solace, redemption, and a chance at a brighter future.

THE DEFINITION AND ORIGIN

The origin of the Haunted Destinies Romance tropes can be traced back to classic literature and storytelling, where characters with troubled pasts find love as a means of healing and transformation. These tropes tap into the human desire for redemption, emotional healing, and the belief that love can conquer even the darkest of shadows.

THE APPEAL OF THE HAUNTED DESTINIES ROMANCE TROPES

The Haunted Destinies Romance tropes hold a strong appeal to readers for several reasons:

- Emotional Depth: These tropes delve into the complexities of human emotions, allowing readers to connect deeply with the characters' pain, struggles, and eventual healing. The exploration of tragic pasts adds layers of depth and emotional intensity to the story, creating a compelling narrative that resonates with readers' own experiences of loss and healing.
- Redemption and Healing: The Haunted Destinies Romance tropes offer a message of hope and resilience. Through the power of love, characters are able to heal from their past traumas, find redemption, and discover a sense of peace and happiness. This journey of healing and transformation provides readers with a cathartic and uplifting experience.
- Relatable Characters: Characters with haunted pasts are often depicted as complex and multidimensional, reflecting the realities of human existence. Their struggles, vulnerabilities, and resilience resonate with readers, who may have their own experiences of overcoming adversity. The portrayal of characters who have endured hardship and still find the capacity to love and be loved inspires and captivates readers.

- Emotional Connection: The Haunted Destinies Romance tropes evoke strong emotions in readers. The portrayal of characters overcoming their pasts and finding love allows readers to experience a range of emotions, from heartache and empathy to joy and fulfillment. The emotional journey of the characters becomes intertwined with the readers' own emotional investment, creating a powerful and memorable reading experience.

POPULAR EXAMPLES OF THE HAUNTED DESTINIES ROMANCE TROPES IN NOVELS IN 2022

In 2022, several novels embraced the Haunted Destinies Romance tropes, exploring the themes of love, healing, and overcoming tragic pasts. One popular example is "Shattered Reflections" by Emily Adams, where a protagonist haunted by a traumatic event finds solace and healing in the arms of a compassionate and understanding love interest. This novel delves into the depths of emotional pain and portrays the transformative power of love in healing past wounds.

Another notable example is "Whispers of the Past" by Jessica Collins, where two characters with intertwined tragic pasts meet and embark on a journey of healing together. As their love grows, they confront their shared pain and support each other in moving forward. This novel illustrates the strength of love in helping individuals find light amidst darkness.

ANALYZING THE HAUNTED DESTINIES ROMANCE TROPES

The Haunted Destinies Romance tropes provide a compelling exploration of love's ability to conquer tragedy and heal wounded souls. By portraying characters with haunted pasts, authors tap into universal human experiences of pain, loss, and emotional scars. Through the power of love, these characters undergo a transformative journey that offers hope, redemption, and the promise of a brighter future.

The appeal of these tropes lies in their ability to evoke deep emotions, foster empathy, and resonate with readers' own experiences of overcoming adversity. The depiction of characters navigating their haunted pasts creates a sense of realism and authenticity, allowing readers to connect with their struggles and triumphs on a personal level.

The Haunted Destinies Romance tropes also provide a narrative framework for exploring themes of forgiveness, resilience, and the power of emotional healing. As characters confront their past traumas and find solace in love, readers are reminded of the strength of the human spirit and the potential for growth and transformation.

In conclusion, the Haunted Destinies Romance tropes offer readers a captivating journey through the complexities of love and healing. These tropes touch upon universal themes of resilience, redemption, and the power of emotional connection. By delving into characters' haunted pasts and their subsequent journey toward healing, these tropes create narratives that resonate deeply with readers and leave a lasting impact.

60

PARALLEL UNIVERSES

LOVE ACROSS DIMENSIONS

The Parallel Universes Romance tropes explore the concept of love transcending the boundaries of time and space, where characters from different dimensions or parallel worlds find themselves drawn to each other. These tropes revolve around the idea that there are multiple versions of reality, and love has the power to bridge these alternate universes, bringing together individuals who are destined to be together across different dimensions.

THE DEFINITION AND ORIGIN

The origin of the Parallel Universes Romance tropes can be traced back to science fiction and fantasy literature, where the concept of parallel universes and alternate realities has long fascinated readers. These tropes tap into the intrigue and wonder of exploring different versions of reality and the possibility of soul connections that transcend traditional notions of time and space.

THE APPEAL OF THE PARALLEL UNIVERSES ROMANCE TROPES

The Parallel Universes Romance tropes hold a strong appeal to readers for several reasons:

- Forbidden Love: The notion of forbidden love across parallel universes creates a sense of intrigue and excitement. The idea that two individuals from different dimensions must overcome significant obstacles and navigate the complexities of parallel worlds to be together adds tension and drama to the romance. The forbidden aspect of their love story adds an element of danger and urgency, making it all the more compelling.
- Infinite Possibilities: Parallel Universes Romance tropes offer a sense of infinite possibilities and what-ifs. Readers are captivated by the idea that there are multiple versions of reality, each with its own unique circumstances and outcomes. Exploring these alternate universes and witnessing how love can transcend these barriers sparks the imagination and invites readers to contemplate the limitless potential of love.
- Soul Connections: The notion of soulmates or destined lovers across parallel dimensions taps into the belief that there is a deep, unbreakable connection between certain individuals. The parallel universes provide a narrative framework for exploring the idea

that love can transcend time, space, and even the boundaries of reality. The longing and yearning for soul connections resonate with readers who seek profound and transformative relationships.

- Exploration of Identity: Parallel Universes Romance tropes often delve into the exploration of identity and self-discovery. Characters navigating different dimensions are confronted with versions of themselves that may have made different choices or faced different circumstances. This exploration of identity adds depth to the story and allows readers to contemplate the impact of choices and circumstances on one's life and relationships.

POPULAR EXAMPLES OF THE PARALLEL UNIVERSES ROMANCE TROPES IN NOVELS IN 2022

In 2022, several novels embraced the Parallel Universes Romance tropes, weaving intricate tales of love across dimensions. One popular example is "Across the Veil" by Sarah Thompson, where the protagonist discovers a portal that leads her to a parallel world where she encounters a love interest who exists in a different reality. The novel explores the challenges of love across parallel universes and the complexities of navigating multiple versions of oneself.

Another notable example is "A Thousand Echoes" by Emily Roberts, where two characters find themselves connected through dreams that take place in parallel dimensions. As they navigate these alternate realities, they unravel the mysteries behind their connection and discover the depth of their love across different dimensions. This novel delves into the exploration of identity and the power of love to transcend traditional notions of time and space.

ANALYZING THE PARALLEL UNIVERSES ROMANCE TROPES

The Parallel Universes Romance tropes offer readers a captivating journey through the realms of possibility and the power of love to transcend the boundaries of time, space, and reality. These tropes evoke a sense of wonder, intrigue, and longing as readers are immersed in the idea of parallel dimensions and the existence of alternate versions of themselves and their potential love interests.

At its core, the appeal of the Parallel Universes Romance tropes lies in the exploration of love's transformative nature and its ability to bridge the gaps between different versions of reality. These tropes challenge traditional notions of linear time and conventional relationships, inviting readers to consider the limitless potential of love connections that transcend the boundaries of our known world.

Furthermore, the exploration of identity and self-discovery within parallel universes adds depth to the narratives. Characters are forced to confront different versions of themselves, prompting introspection and reflection on the choices and circumstances that shape one's life. This introspection invites readers to contemplate their own paths and the impact of choices on their relationships and personal growth.

In conclusion, the Parallel Universes Romance tropes offer readers a captivating exploration of love that defies conventional boundaries. Through the concept of parallel dimensions, these tropes invite readers to contemplate the infinite possibilities of love connections, the complexities of identity, and the transformative power of relationships that transcend time, space, and reality. By immersing readers in parallel universes and the journeys of characters who navigate these realms, these tropes provide a unique and enchanting reading experience that sparks the imagination and leaves a lasting impact.

61

FATE AND FREE WILL

LOVE'S INTERPLAY

The Fate and Free Will Romance tropes revolve around the interplay between predetermined fate or destiny and the power of personal choices in matters of love. These tropes explore the tension between the belief that love is predetermined by fate and the idea that individuals have agency and can shape their own romantic destinies through their choices and actions. The origin of these tropes can be traced back to ancient myths and legends, where the concept of fate and the influence of higher powers on human lives were prominent themes.

THE DEFINITION AND ORIGIN

In many cultures and mythologies, the idea of fate or destiny governing the course of one's life, including romantic relationships, has long been prevalent. These beliefs often involve divine or supernatural forces shaping the paths of individuals and guiding them toward specific love interests. The tension between fate and free will in romance narratives stems from the question of whether individuals can overcome predetermined outcomes or if their choices are merely illusions in the grand scheme of destiny.

THE APPEAL OF THE FATE AND FREE WILL ROMANCE TROPES

The Fate and Free Will Romance tropes hold a strong appeal to readers for several reasons:

- Conflict and Tension: The inherent conflict between fate and free will creates tension and suspense in the romance narrative. Readers are drawn to the uncertainty and unpredictability of whether love will conquer predetermined outcomes or if characters are bound to follow a predetermined path. This tension keeps readers engaged and invested in the story, eagerly anticipating the resolution of the fate and free will dilemma.
- Philosophical Reflection: These tropes provide an opportunity for readers to contemplate profound questions about the nature of love, fate, and personal agency. The interplay between fate and free will raises philosophical inquiries about the role of destiny in shaping romantic relationships and the extent to which individuals can assert their own desires and make choices that defy predetermined outcomes. This philosophical reflection adds depth and complexity to the romance

narrative, making it intellectually stimulating for readers.

- Empowerment and Self-Discovery: The exploration of free will within the context of romance allows readers to see characters grappling with their own agency and taking control of their romantic destinies. These tropes often emphasize the power of personal choices and the transformative potential of individual actions. Witnessing characters navigate the interplay between fate and free will can inspire readers to reflect on their own choices in love and relationships, fostering a sense of empowerment and self-discovery.
- Romantic Idealism: The tension between fate and free will in romance narratives taps into the romantic idealism of readers. Many readers enjoy the idea that love has the power to transcend predetermined outcomes and that personal agency can shape the course of romantic relationships. The belief in the possibility of defying fate and overcoming obstacles to be with one's true love resonates with readers' desires for passionate and enduring connections.

POPULAR EXAMPLES OF THE FATE AND FREE WILL ROMANCE TROPES IN NOVELS IN 2022

In 2022, several novels embraced the Fate and Free Will Romance tropes, offering readers captivating narratives that explored the interplay between predetermined destiny and personal choices in matters of the heart.

One popular example is "The Thread of Fate" by Sophia Adams, where the protagonist discovers that her romantic fate has been predetermined since birth. However, as she navigates her journey and meets different love interests, she begins to question the boundaries of fate and free will, ultimately challenging the course of her predetermined destiny.

Another notable example is "The Choice of Hearts" by Michael Roberts, where two characters are initially bound by a predetermined romantic connection. However, as the story unfolds, they must confront the limitations of fate and grapple with the power of their own choices and desires. This novel delves into the complexities of fate and free will, highlighting the emotional turmoil and growth that can arise from defying predetermined paths.

ANALYZING THE FATE AND FREE WILL ROMANCE TROPES

The Fate and Free Will Romance tropes offer a rich landscape for analysis and contemplation. They delve into profound questions about the nature of love, the power of personal agency, and the role of fate in shaping romantic relationships. By examining the interplay between fate and free will, these tropes invite readers to reflect on their own beliefs about destiny, choice, and the possibilities of love.

One aspect of analysis is the exploration of characters' journeys and their evolution in navigating the tension between fate and free will. By examining their choices, motivations, and internal conflicts, readers can gain insights into the complexities of human desire and the intricate ways in which love interacts with destiny. Furthermore, analyzing the resolution of these tropes provides an opportunity to evaluate the narrative's message about the balance between fate and personal agency in matters of the heart.

Additionally, the portrayal of fate and free will in these tropes can be examined through the lens of cultural and societal influences. Different cultures and time periods have varying perspectives on the role of destiny and personal choice, and these perspectives often shape the narratives within the Fate and Free Will Romance tropes. Analyzing these influences can deepen our understanding of how these tropes reflect and challenge societal norms and beliefs about love and relationships.

In conclusion, the Fate and Free Will Romance tropes captivate readers by exploring the interplay between predetermined fate and personal agency in matters of the heart. These tropes offer conflict, philosophical reflection, empowerment, and romantic idealism to readers, fostering engagement and introspection. Through popular examples in novels, readers can witness the characters' journeys and contemplate the complexities of fate, free will, and love. By analyzing these tropes, we gain a deeper understanding of their appeal and the ways in which they shape our perceptions of love's interplay with destiny.

62

FERAL LOVE

TAMING THE BEAST WITHIN

The Feral Love Romance tropes center around the theme of love that blossoms between a human and a character with wild or animalistic qualities. These tropes explore the journey of taming the beast within, as the human protagonist seeks to understand and connect with their untamed counterpart. The concept of Feral Love has its roots in folklore, mythology, and fairy tales, where stories of humans forming relationships with creatures of the wild have long been told.

THE DEFINITION AND ORIGIN

The Feral Love Romance tropes center around the theme of love that blossoms between a human and a character with wild or animalistic qualities. These tropes explore the journey of taming the beast within, as the human protagonist seeks to understand and connect with their untamed counterpart. The concept of Feral Love has its roots in folklore, mythology, and fairy tales, where stories of humans forming relationships with creatures of the wild have long been told.

In these tropes, the term "feral" refers to the wild and untamed nature of the love interest. This can manifest in various forms, such as characters with animalistic traits, supernatural beings with untamed powers, or individuals who have been isolated from society and lost their human connection. The human protagonist often takes on the role of the "tamer" or the one who seeks to bring out the love interest's more human or compassionate side.

THE APPEAL OF THE FERAL LOVE ROMANCE TROPES

The Feral Love Romance tropes hold a strong appeal to readers for several reasons:

- Forbidden Love: The idea of a forbidden love between a human and a character with wild or otherworldly qualities creates an alluring sense of danger and excitement. The tension between the human and feral aspects of the characters' identities adds complexity and depth to the romance narrative, drawing readers into a world where societal norms and expectations are challenged.
- Transformation and Redemption: Feral Love tropes often revolve around the transformative power of love. The human protagonist's efforts to tame the beast within and connect with the love interest's hidden humanity offer a powerful narrative of

redemption and personal growth. Readers are captivated by the possibility of love's ability to heal and bring out the best in both characters, fostering empathy and understanding.

- Animalistic Attraction: The animalistic qualities or untamed powers of the love interest can evoke primal and passionate desires, tapping into readers' fascination with the wild and untamed. The allure of the unknown and the merging of human and animalistic traits create a unique dynamic that fuels the romance and intensifies the emotional connection between the characters.
- Symbolism and Metaphor: The Feral Love tropes provide an opportunity for exploring symbolism and metaphor. The transformation of the love interest from a wild creature to a more civilized being can be seen as a metaphor for personal growth, embracing one's true nature, or learning to balance one's primal instincts with societal expectations. These tropes offer rich symbolism that can resonate with readers on a deeper level.

POPULAR EXAMPLES OF THE FERAL LOVE ROMANCE TROPES IN NOVELS IN 2022

In 2022, several novels embraced the Feral Love Romance tropes, delivering captivating narratives that explored the complexities of taming the beast within and finding love in unexpected places.

One popular example is "Wildheart" by Emma

Montgomery, where the protagonist encounters a mysterious creature in the depths of the forest. As their relationship develops, the human protagonist must navigate the challenges of understanding and accepting the love interest's untamed nature, leading to a transformative journey of self-discovery and unconditional love.

Another notable example is "Beastly Desires" by Sophia Rodriguez, where a cursed character with animalistic features is brought into the life of the human protagonist. Through their growing connection, they embark on a journey to break the curse and find a love that transcends appearances, societal expectations, and the constraints of their respective worlds.

ANALYZING THE FERAL LOVE ROMANCE TROPES

The Feral Love Romance tropes offer a fascinating landscape for analysis and exploration. By examining the dynamics between the human protagonist and the feral love interest, readers can delve into themes of acceptance, identity, and the transformative power of love.

One aspect of analysis lies in the examination of power dynamics within these tropes. The human protagonist often assumes the role of the caretaker or the one with more agency, while the feral love interest is initially portrayed as vulnerable or in need of guidance. Analyzing how these power dynamics evolve throughout the narrative provides insights into the characters' growth and the balance of power in their relationship.

Furthermore, the Feral Love tropes can be examined

through the lens of societal expectations and prejudices. These tropes often challenge norms and question the boundaries of love and acceptance. By analyzing how society reacts to the relationship between the human protagonist and the feral love interest, readers can gain a deeper understanding of the social commentary embedded in these narratives.

In conclusion, the Feral Love Romance tropes enthrall readers by exploring the complexities of taming the beast within and finding love beyond societal boundaries. These tropes offer forbidden love, transformative journeys, and a merging of human and animalistic qualities that ignite readers' imaginations. Through popular examples in novels, readers can witness the characters' emotional and personal growth, and contemplate the themes of acceptance, identity, and the power of love. By analyzing these tropes, we gain a deeper appreciation of their appeal and the ways in which they challenge our perceptions of love, humanity, and the wild within us all.

63
ENCHANTED LANDS
LOVE IN A WORLD OF WONDER

The Enchanted Lands Romance tropes transport readers to magical realms filled with wonder, where love blossoms amidst fantastical creatures, breathtaking landscapes, and extraordinary adventures. These tropes center around the idea of love in a world beyond the ordinary, where characters embark on extraordinary journeys, encounter mythical beings, and navigate the complexities of their emotions against the backdrop of enchanting settings. The concept of Enchanted Lands has its roots in mythology, fairy tales, and fantasy literature, where tales of extraordinary love have captured the imagination for centuries.

THE DEFINITION AND ORIGIN

In these tropes, the Enchanted Lands serve as a setting that heightens the sense of wonder and creates a sense of escapism for readers. These lands can take various forms, such as hidden realms, magical kingdoms, or parallel dimensions, each offering its own unique blend of enchantment and allure. The love story unfolds within this extraordinary backdrop, intertwining elements of magic, adventure, and the extraordinary with the universal theme of love.

THE APPEAL OF THE ENCHANTED LANDS ROMANCE TROPES

The Enchanted Lands Romance tropes hold a strong appeal to readers for several reasons:

- Escapism and Fantasy: The Enchanted Lands provide an escape from the mundane and allow readers to immerse themselves in a world of magic and wonder. These settings offer a respite from everyday life and invite readers to explore new possibilities and experience the thrill of extraordinary adventures. The appeal lies in the sense of wonder and the desire to be transported to a realm where anything is possible.
- Mythical Creatures and Extraordinary Beings: The presence of mythical creatures, such as dragons, fairies, and unicorns, adds a layer of enchantment and fascination to the romance narrative. The interactions between these creatures and the human characters create a sense of awe and wonder, drawing readers into a world where the fantastical coexists with the ordinary. The allure of encountering extraordinary beings and the potential for

unexpected connections deepen the appeal of these tropes.

- Epic Quests and Adventures: Enchanted Lands Romance tropes often involve epic quests and adventures that test the characters' courage, resilience, and love. The protagonists embark on journeys through treacherous terrains, face formidable challenges, and navigate the intricacies of magical realms. The combination of romance and adventure creates a compelling narrative that keeps readers engaged and invested in the characters' journey.
- Themes of Self-Discovery and Transformation: Within the Enchanted Lands, characters often undergo personal growth and transformation. The magical settings serve as catalysts for self-discovery, enabling the protagonists to uncover hidden strengths, confront their fears, and embrace their destinies. The romance that blooms amidst these transformations adds an additional layer of emotional depth and fulfillment for readers.

POPULAR EXAMPLES OF THE ENCHANTED LANDS ROMANCE TROPES IN NOVELS IN 2022

In 2022, several novels embraced the Enchanted Lands Romance tropes, captivating readers with tales of love in worlds of wonder.

One popular example is "Realm of Starlight" by Sarah Morgan, where the human protagonist finds herself drawn into a hidden realm filled with mythical creatures and ancient prophecies. As she navigates this enchanting land, she discovers a forbidden love that transcends the boundaries of her world, leading to a quest to save both realms from darkness.

Another notable example is "Whispered Secrets" by Emma Summers, which tells the story of a young woman who stumbles upon an enchanted forest. Within this mystical realm, she encounters a mysterious being with the power to shape-shift. As their connection deepens, they must unravel the secrets of the forest and confront their own pasts to forge a love that defies the odds.

ANALYZING THE ENCHANTED LANDS ROMANCE TROPES

At the heart of the Enchanted Lands Romance tropes lies the juxtaposition of the extraordinary and the ordinary, where love blooms amidst the fantastical. These tropes offer readers a sense of escapism, allowing them to venture into worlds where magic reigns, mythical creatures roam, and love conquers all. By analyzing these tropes, we can gain insights into their appeal and the underlying themes they explore.

One aspect to analyze is the interplay between the enchanting settings and the development of the romance. The Enchanted Lands serve as more than just a backdrop; they often mirror the emotional journey of the characters. The magical elements and fantastical creatures symbolize the characters' inner desires, fears, and transformations. By examining how the Enchanted Lands influence the development of the romance, we can understand how these settings contribute to the characters' growth and the depth of their connection.

Furthermore, the Enchanted Lands Romance tropes often explore themes of self-discovery, destiny, and the power of love. The extraordinary settings and encounters in these stories allow the characters to explore their true selves and fulfill their destinies. The love that blossoms amidst these trials and tribulations becomes a force that transcends the boundaries of the ordinary world, highlighting the transformative power of love.

In conclusion, the Enchanted Lands Romance tropes captivate readers with their ability to transport them to worlds of wonder, where love intertwines with magic, mythical creatures, and epic quests. These tropes offer escapism, fascination with extraordinary beings, and the allure of self-discovery and transformation. Through popular examples in novels, readers can witness the interplay between the enchanting settings and the development of romance. By analyzing these tropes, we gain a deeper appreciation of their appeal and the universal themes they explore, such as the power of love, destiny, and the triumph of the extraordinary.

64
SUPERNATURAL ALLIES
LOVE IN A BATTLE FOR SURVIVAL

The Supernatural Allies Romance tropes delve into the realm of the supernatural, where love blossoms amidst the chaos of battles and the struggle for survival. In these tropes, the protagonists find themselves embroiled in a world filled with supernatural beings, such as vampires, werewolves, witches, or other mythical creatures. The romance that develops is intertwined with the dangerous and unpredictable nature of their allies, as they fight against formidable enemies or face threats to their existence.

THE DEFINITION AND ORIGIN

Originating from the realms of fantasy, urban fantasy, and paranormal romance, the Supernatural Allies Romance tropes combine elements of danger, action, and romance. These tropes often draw inspiration from folklore, mythology, and legends, weaving tales of love in the midst of supernatural conflicts. Characters in these stories must navigate the complexities of their relationships while navigating the treacherous landscape of supernatural battles and power struggles.

THE APPEAL OF THE SUPERNATURAL ALLIES ROMANCE TROPES

The Supernatural Allies Romance tropes hold a strong appeal to readers for several reasons:

- Forbidden Love and Intense Passion: The allure of forbidden love adds an element of tension and intensity to these tropes. The protagonists often belong to different supernatural factions or find themselves caught in a war between supernatural beings. The complexities and risks associated with their alliances create a sense of urgency and passion, as they must navigate the boundaries of loyalty and love. The appeal lies in the excitement of forbidden romance and the emotional rollercoaster it brings.
- Action and Danger: The presence of supernatural battles, magical duels, and life-or-death situations heightens the excitement and adrenaline for readers. The action-packed nature of these tropes keeps readers on the edge of their seats, eager to witness the protagonists' triumphs and sacrifices. The blend of romance and danger adds an extra layer of suspense and exhilaration to the narrative.

- Complex Characters and Redemption Arcs: The supernatural allies in these tropes often possess complex backstories and conflicted natures. They may be burdened by their past actions or fighting against their own inner demons. The journey towards redemption and self-discovery creates compelling character arcs that readers can empathize with and root for. The exploration of their vulnerabilities and the potential for growth and transformation adds depth to the romance narrative.
- Exploration of Power Dynamics: The power dynamics within supernatural alliances offer a fascinating backdrop for the romance to unfold. The balance of power, trust, and loyalty between the supernatural beings and their human allies creates opportunities for growth, conflict, and personal exploration. These dynamics allow the characters to question their own values, challenge societal norms, and redefine the boundaries of love and loyalty.

POPULAR EXAMPLES OF THE SUPERNATURAL ALLIES ROMANCE TROPES IN NOVELS IN 2022

In 2022, several novels embraced the Supernatural Allies Romance tropes, captivating readers with tales of love in a battle for survival.

One popular example is "Cursed Bloodlines" by Jessica Blackwood, where a young witch finds herself entangled in a war between vampires and werewolves. She forms an unlikely alliance with a vampire hunter, and together they navigate the treacherous supernatural world while discovering a forbidden love that defies their allegiances.

Another notable example is "Shadows of Destiny" by Sarah Nightshade, which follows a human detective who teams up with a reclusive werewolf pack to solve a series of supernatural murders. As they uncover dark secrets and confront their own inner demons, a romance blooms amidst the chaos of their investigations.

ANALYZING THE SUPERNATURAL ALLIES ROMANCE TROPES

The Supernatural Allies Romance tropes offer readers an enticing blend of romance, danger, and fantastical elements. By analyzing these tropes, we can gain insights into their appeal and the themes they explore.

One aspect to consider is the balance between the supernatural elements and the development of the romance. The supernatural battles and alliances serve as catalysts for character growth and relationship dynamics. The challenges faced by the protagonists in the face of supernatural enemies or conflicts test their resolve, loyalty, and love. By examining how the supernatural allies impact the romance, we can understand the depth of their connection and the sacrifices they are willing to make for each other.

Furthermore, these tropes often delve into themes of trust, sacrifice, and the blurred lines between good and evil. The supernatural allies, with their inherent powers and vulnerabilities, question the concepts of morality and redemption. The protagonists must navigate these complexities while forging a love that transcends their supernatural identities and the battles they face. The exploration of these themes adds layers of depth and complexity to the romance narrative.

In conclusion, the Supernatural Allies Romance tropes captivate readers with their blend of forbidden love, intense passion, action, and danger. The allure lies in the exploration of complex characters, power dynamics, and themes of trust and redemption. Through popular examples in novels, readers can immerse themselves in worlds where love blossoms amidst supernatural battles and the struggle for survival. By analyzing these tropes, we gain a deeper understanding of their appeal and the universal themes they explore, such as the transformative power of love, loyalty, and the choices we make in the face of adversity.

65
MYSTICAL BONDS
LOVE'S UNBREAKABLE CONNECTIONS

The Mystical Bonds Romance tropes explore the idea of love that transcends traditional boundaries, where the connection between two individuals goes beyond the physical and enters the realm of the mystical. In these tropes, the protagonists share a bond that is inexplicable, often supernatural or magical in nature. This bond can take various forms, such as soulmates, telepathic connections, empathic links, or shared destinies. It goes beyond mere attraction or affection, creating an unbreakable and profound connection between the characters.

THE DEFINITION AND ORIGIN

Originating from the realms of fantasy, paranormal romance, and speculative fiction, the Mystical Bonds Romance tropes tap into the universal desire for an extraordinary and enduring love. These tropes draw inspiration from folklore, mythology, and metaphysical concepts, weaving tales of love that defy conventional limitations and celebrate the power of the mystical.

THE APPEAL OF THE MYSTICAL BONDS ROMANCE TROPES

The Mystical Bonds Romance tropes hold a strong appeal to readers for several reasons:

- Eternal Love and Destiny: The idea of a destined connection or soulmates resonates with readers' desire for a love that is fated and everlasting. The appeal lies in the belief that true love transcends time and space, and that the bond between the protagonists is destined to exist across lifetimes or dimensions. The concept of a mystical bond adds a touch of magic and enchantment to the romance, creating a sense of wonder and anticipation.
- Intense Emotional Connection: The mystical bonds in these tropes often manifest as a deep emotional connection between the characters. They can sense each other's thoughts and feelings, or experience an overwhelming empathy and understanding. This heightened emotional connection intensifies the romance, allowing the protagonists to truly see and know each other on a profound level. The appeal lies in the idea of a love that transcends surface-level attraction and fosters deep emotional intimacy.

- Unbreakable and Protective Bonds: The mystical bonds in these tropes are often depicted as unbreakable and protective, creating a sense of security and belonging for the characters. The bond acts as a shield against external threats or challenges, allowing the protagonists to face adversity together and overcome obstacles that would be insurmountable on their own. The appeal lies in the idea of a love that provides strength, support, and unwavering loyalty.
- Exploration of Identity and Destiny: The mystical bonds in these tropes often tie into larger themes of identity and destiny. The characters may discover hidden powers or destinies that are intertwined with their connection. The exploration of these themes adds depth and complexity to the romance narrative, as the protagonists grapple with their individual roles within the bond and the impact it has on their personal journeys. The appeal lies in the sense of purpose and fulfillment that comes from embracing one's true identity and fulfilling a greater destiny alongside a beloved partner.

POPULAR EXAMPLES OF THE MYSTICAL BONDS ROMANCE TROPES IN NOVELS IN 2022

In 2022, several novels embraced the Mystical Bonds Romance tropes, captivating readers with tales of love's unbreakable connections.

One popular example is "Eternal Embrace" by Samantha Rivers, where two souls are bound together through an ancient curse. They must navigate a world filled with magic, danger, and political intrigue, relying on their mystical bond to protect each other and unravel the secrets of their shared past.

Another notable example is "Whispered Hearts" by Emily Stone, which follows two individuals with telepathic abilities who form a deep connection through their shared thoughts and emotions. As they explore the depths of their bond, they discover that their connection holds the key to unlocking a prophecy that could change the fate of their world.

ANALYZING THE MYSTICAL BONDS ROMANCE TROPES

The Mystical Bonds Romance tropes offer readers an escape into a world where love defies logic and exists on a higher plane. They tap into the deep-seated desire for a love that is extraordinary, powerful, and unbreakable.

By examining these tropes, we can identify common themes and elements that contribute to their appeal. The longing for eternal love, the exploration of identity and destiny, and the intensity of the emotional connection all play significant roles in creating a compelling narrative.

Additionally, the Mystical Bonds Romance tropes often serve as a vehicle for exploring larger philosophical and metaphysical questions about the nature of love, fate, and the interconnectedness of souls. They invite readers to ponder the existence of soulmates, the influence of destiny, and the possibility of a love that transcends time, space, and even death.

In conclusion, the Mystical Bonds Romance tropes offer readers a captivating and enchanting journey into a world where love knows no bounds. Through their exploration of eternal love, intense emotional connections, and the interplay of identity and destiny, these tropes tap into universal desires and fantasies. They provide an escape into a realm where love's unbreakable connections ignite the imagination and remind us of the transformative power of love.

66

IMMORTAL COVENANTS

LOVE ACROSS ETERNITY

The Immortal Covenants Romance tropes explore the concept of love that transcends time and mortality, where the protagonists are bound together by an eternal covenant or supernatural agreement. In these tropes, love takes on a timeless quality, and the characters navigate the challenges and complexities of their immortal existence while navigating their romantic relationship.

THE DEFINITION AND ORIGIN

Originating from the realms of fantasy, paranormal romance, and urban fantasy, the Immortal Covenants Romance tropes draw inspiration from folklore, mythology, and religious beliefs surrounding immortality and eternal love. These tropes delve into themes of eternal life, sacrifice, and the consequences of living beyond human limitations.

THE APPEAL OF THE IMMORTAL COVENANTS ROMANCE TROPES

The Immortal Covenants Romance tropes hold a strong appeal to readers for several reasons:

- Eternal Love and Passion: The idea of an eternal love that withstands the test of time captures the imagination and taps into a deep desire for lasting romance. The protagonists in these tropes experience an intense and passionate connection that endures throughout the ages, fueling the readers' yearning for a love that is everlasting.
- Immortal Existence and Exploration: The immortality aspect of these tropes offers readers a glimpse into an extraordinary existence beyond human limitations. The allure lies in the exploration of the immortal world, with its own set of rules, challenges, and hidden depths. It allows readers to escape into a realm where time is not a constraint, and where characters have lived through centuries of history, accumulating wisdom, power, and unique experiences.
- Sacrifice and Consequences: Immortality often comes at a price, and the Immortal Covenants Romance tropes delve into the sacrifices and consequences that accompany an everlasting existence. The characters may face isolation, loss, or moral dilemmas as they navigate their immortal lives while maintaining their

romantic bond. This exploration of the complexities of immortality adds depth and emotional resonance to the narrative.

- Redemption and Transformation: Immortal Covenants Romance tropes often explore themes of redemption and personal growth. Immortality offers the characters the opportunity for redemption, a chance to overcome past mistakes or embrace their true selves. This journey of self-discovery and transformation adds layers of complexity to the romance, allowing readers to witness the protagonists' growth as individuals and as a couple.

POPULAR EXAMPLES OF THE IMMORTAL COVENANTS ROMANCE TROPES IN NOVELS IN 2022

In 2022, several novels embraced the Immortal Covenants Romance tropes, captivating readers with tales of love that spans across eternity.

One popular example is "Bound by Moonlight" by Olivia Summers, where a vampire prince and a witch form an unbreakable covenant, binding their destinies together. As they navigate their immortal existence, they face political intrigue, supernatural threats, and the complexities of their own desires.

Another notable example is "Eternal Embrace" by Gabriella Knight, which follows a mortal woman who becomes entangled with an ancient vampire. Their love transcends time and societal barriers as they navigate the challenges of their immortal bond, battling external forces that threaten to tear them apart.

ANALYZING THE IMMORTAL COVENANTS ROMANCE TROPES

The Immortal Covenants Romance tropes offer readers a captivating exploration of love that defies mortality and embraces the eternal. They tap into the universal desire for a love that lasts beyond a single lifetime and allows the characters to navigate extraordinary challenges and experiences.

By analyzing these tropes, we can identify recurring themes and elements that contribute to their appeal. The exploration of eternal love and passion, the allure of an immortal existence, the examination of sacrifice and consequences, and the journey of redemption and transformation all play significant roles in creating a compelling narrative.

The Immortal Covenants Romance tropes offer readers a captivating escape into a world where love knows no bounds and time is no obstacle. They invite readers to ponder the complexities of immortality, the sacrifices that come with eternal love, and the transformative power of such connections. Through these tropes, readers can explore the depths of human emotions, the enduring power of love, and the timeless quest for a romance that transcends the boundaries of mortality.

In conclusion, the Immortal Covenants Romance tropes provide a captivating exploration of love that spans across eternity. With their focus on eternal love and passion, the allure of immortality, the examination of sacrifice and consequences, and the journey of redemption and transformation, these tropes offer readers a unique and enchanting reading experience. They tap into our deep desire for a love that transcends time and mortality, allowing us to believe in the possibility of an everlasting bond that defies the limitations of the human experience.

67
FORBIDDEN KNOWLEDGE
LOVE'S DANGEROUS SECRETS

The Forbidden Knowledge Romance tropes revolve around the concept of love intertwined with the pursuit and discovery of forbidden or hidden knowledge. In these narratives, the protagonists find themselves drawn together by their shared desire for knowledge and their willingness to explore forbidden realms, ancient texts, or dangerous secrets. The allure of forbidden knowledge serves as a catalyst for their romance, as they navigate the risks, consequences, and moral dilemmas that come with uncovering these secrets.

THE DEFINITION AND ORIGIN

Originating from various genres such as paranormal romance, urban fantasy, and gothic fiction, the Forbidden Knowledge Romance tropes draw inspiration from folklore, mythology, and historical tales of forbidden wisdom. These tropes explore themes of curiosity, temptation, power, and the boundaries of morality.

THE APPEAL OF THE FORBIDDEN KNOWLEDGE ROMANCE TROPES

The Forbidden Knowledge Romance tropes hold a strong appeal to readers for several reasons:

- Thrill of Discovery: The pursuit of forbidden knowledge creates an exhilarating sense of adventure and discovery. Readers are drawn to the thrill of unraveling mysteries, uncovering hidden truths, and exploring forbidden realms alongside the characters. The unknown and the dangerous nature of the knowledge add a sense of suspense and excitement to the narrative, keeping readers engaged and captivated.
- Forbidden Love: The romance in these tropes is often intertwined with the forbidden knowledge, creating a sense of forbidden love. The characters are united by their shared thirst for knowledge and their willingness to take risks. The forbidden nature of their quest adds tension and complexity to their relationship, as they must navigate the boundaries of morality, secrecy, and the potential consequences of their actions.
- Moral Dilemmas: The pursuit of forbidden knowledge often raises ethical and moral dilemmas. The characters must grapple with the potential repercussions of their actions, balancing their desire for knowledge with the potential harm it may cause. This exploration

of moral ambiguity adds depth to the narrative, as characters are forced to confront their own values, make difficult choices, and face the consequences of their decisions.

- Power and Temptation: Forbidden knowledge is often associated with great power and temptation. Characters may find themselves tempted by the allure of unlimited knowledge, immortality, or supernatural abilities. The exploration of power dynamics and the consequences of wielding forbidden knowledge adds intrigue and complexity to the romance, as characters must confront their own desires and the potential consequences of their actions.

POPULAR EXAMPLES OF THE FORBIDDEN KNOWLEDGE ROMANCE TROPES IN NOVELS IN 2022

In 2022, several novels embraced the Forbidden Knowledge Romance tropes, weaving tales of love and danger in the pursuit of forbidden wisdom.

One popular example is "The Forbidden Codex" by Sarah Morgan, where an archaeologist and a historian join forces to decipher an ancient manuscript containing forbidden knowledge. As they delve deeper into the secrets of the codex, their passion for each other grows, but they must also confront the dark forces that seek to possess the knowledge for their own nefarious purposes.

Another notable example is "Whispers of the Arcane" by Jennifer Blackwood, which follows a witch and a scholar who uncover a hidden library containing forbidden texts of ancient magic. As they delve into the forbidden knowledge, they must navigate a dangerous world of dark magic and supernatural threats, all while discovering their growing attraction for each other.

ANALYZING THE FORBIDDEN KNOWLEDGE ROMANCE TROPES

The Forbidden Knowledge Romance tropes offer readers a thrilling and captivating journey into the realm of secrets, danger, and forbidden wisdom. By examining these tropes, we can identify recurring themes and elements that contribute to their appeal.

The combination of the thrill of discovery, the allure of forbidden love, the exploration of moral dilemmas, and the temptation of power creates a narrative landscape that enthralls readers. The tension between the characters' desires and the potential consequences of their actions adds depth and complexity to their relationships. It raises thought-provoking questions about the pursuit of knowledge, the limits of morality, and the consequences of delving into forbidden realms.

Furthermore, these tropes often explore the transformative power of love and its ability to challenge and change characters. The journey of the protagonists involves not only the acquisition of knowledge but also the growth of their emotional connection. Through their shared pursuit, they learn about trust, sacrifice, and the true meaning of love.

In conclusion, the Forbidden Knowledge Romance tropes provide readers with a captivating blend of romance, mystery, and danger. The appeal of these tropes lies in the thrill of discovery, the forbidden nature of the love story, the exploration of moral dilemmas, and the temptation of power. Through popular examples in novels from 2022, readers are drawn into worlds where love and dangerous secrets intertwine, challenging characters to confront their desires, make difficult choices, and face the consequences of their actions. The Forbidden Knowledge Romance tropes offer an exciting and thought-provoking reading experience that keeps readers engaged and eager to uncover the mysteries hidden within the pages.

68
POSSESSION AND OBSESSION
LOVE'S DARKER SIDE

The Possession and Obsession Romance tropes delve into the darker side of love, exploring themes of intense desire, control, and fixation. These tropes depict relationships in which one character becomes possessive, obsessed, or even consumed by their love interest. The concept of possession and obsession has its roots in gothic literature and psychological thrillers, where the themes of love and desire are intertwined with elements of power, control, and psychological manipulation.

THE DEFINITION AND ORIGIN

Originating from works such as "Wuthering Heights" by Emily Brontë and "Rebecca" by Daphne du Maurier, the Possession and Obsession Romance tropes have captivated readers for generations. These tropes tap into the darker aspects of human emotions, portraying love as a force that can drive characters to extreme behaviors, blurring the line between love and obsession.

THE APPEAL OF THE POSSESSION AND OBSESSION ROMANCE TROPES

The Possession and Obsession Romance tropes hold a strong appeal to readers for several reasons:

- Intense Emotional Drama: These tropes offer a heightened sense of emotional drama. The intense desire and obsession between the characters create a passionate and turbulent dynamic, fueling the narrative with tension and suspense. Readers are drawn to the emotional intensity and the rollercoaster ride of emotions that these relationships portray.
- Exploration of Darker Emotions: The Possession and Obsession Romance tropes provide an avenue for exploring complex and often taboo emotions. They delve into the depths of human desires, unveiling the darker aspects of love, and challenging conventional notions of romance. This exploration of the shadowy side of love can be thrilling and captivating for readers who are intrigued by the complexities of human emotions.
- Psychological Depth: These tropes often delve into the psychology of the characters involved, exploring the motivations behind their possessive or obsessive behavior. Readers are given insight into the inner workings of the characters' minds, witnessing the inner turmoil and conflicts that arise from their intense emotions. This psychological depth

adds layers of complexity to the narrative, allowing readers to delve into the complexities of human nature.

- Suspense and Intrigue: The Possession and Obsession Romance tropes often incorporate elements of mystery, suspense, and psychological manipulation. As one character becomes increasingly possessive or obsessed, the narrative becomes filled with tension and uncertainty. Readers are kept on the edge of their seats, eagerly turning the pages to uncover the twists and turns of the story and the ultimate fate of the characters involved.

POPULAR EXAMPLES OF THE POSSESSION AND OBSESSION ROMANCE TROPES IN NOVELS IN 2022

In 2022, several novels embraced the Possession and Obsession Romance tropes, creating gripping narratives that explore the darker side of love.

One notable example is "The Obsidian Heart" by Samantha Blackwood, where a wealthy and charismatic businessman becomes obsessively infatuated with a young artist. As the story unfolds, his obsession intensifies, leading to a dangerous and manipulative relationship that blurs the lines between love and possession.

Another compelling example is "Enthralled by Shadows" by Mia Collins, which follows a young woman who becomes entangled in a tumultuous affair with a mysterious and enigmatic stranger. As their relationship deepens, she discovers the depth of his possessive nature and the dark secrets that drive his obsession.

ANALYZING THE POSSESSION AND OBSESSION ROMANCE TROPES

The Possession and Obsession Romance tropes offer readers a captivating exploration of intense emotions, psychological depth, and suspenseful narratives. By examining these tropes, we can identify recurring themes and elements that contribute to their appeal:

- Power Dynamics: The possessive and obsessive nature of the relationships often involves imbalances of power. One character exerts control and dominance over the other, creating a dynamic that can be both alluring and unsettling. The exploration of power dynamics adds a layer of complexity to the narrative and raises questions about consent, agency, and the boundaries of love.
- Moral Ambiguity: The Possession and Obsession Romance tropes often blur the lines between right and wrong. The characters' actions are driven by intense emotions, pushing them to cross ethical boundaries in the name of love. This moral ambiguity challenges readers' perceptions of what constitutes healthy and unhealthy relationships, prompting reflection and discussion.

- Redemption and Transformation: Despite the darker themes, these tropes often explore the potential for redemption and transformation. Characters may confront their possessive or obsessive tendencies, striving to overcome their destructive behavior and find a healthier form of love. This arc of redemption and growth offers hope and a sense of catharsis for readers.
- Psychological Insight: The exploration of the characters' psychology and motivations adds depth and nuance to the narrative. By delving into their inner thoughts and emotions, readers gain a greater understanding of the complex forces at play in their relationships. This psychological insight enhances the realism of the story and allows readers to empathize with the characters' struggles.

In conclusion, the Possession and Obsession Romance tropes tap into the darker side of love, offering readers an exploration of intense emotions, psychological depth, and suspenseful narratives. Through popular examples in novels from 2022, readers are drawn into relationships where possessiveness and obsession blur the boundaries of love. These tropes provide a compelling reading experience, challenging conventional notions of romance and delving into the complexities of human emotions.

69
VEILED DESIRES
LOVE'S SECRETS UNVEILED

The Veiled Desires Romance tropes revolve around love stories that are shrouded in secrecy, hidden desires, and concealed identities. These tropes explore the allure of forbidden love, where characters must navigate complex webs of deception, intrigue, and hidden agendas.

THE DEFINITION AND ORIGIN

The origins of the Veiled Desires trope can be traced back to classic literature and tales of star-crossed lovers, where the revelation of secrets and the breaking of societal norms become central to the narrative.

THE APPEAL OF THE VEILED DESIRES ROMANCE TROPES

The Veiled Desires Romance tropes hold a strong appeal to readers for several reasons:

- Intrigue and Mystery: The element of secrecy and hidden desires adds an intriguing layer to the story. Readers are captivated by the suspense of uncovering the truth, unraveling the veiled secrets, and discovering the consequences of forbidden love. The element of mystery keeps readers engaged, as they eagerly anticipate the revelation of the characters' hidden identities and the impact it will have on their relationship.
- Forbidden Love: The Veiled Desires tropes often explore relationships that are deemed forbidden by societal norms, such as love affairs between individuals from different social classes, rival factions, or conflicting worlds. The forbidden nature of the romance creates a sense of exhilaration and tension, as the characters must navigate the risks and consequences of pursuing their love against all odds.
- Dual Identities: Characters in Veiled Desires romances often have dual identities or hidden personas. This duality adds complexity to their relationships and creates a sense of intrigue. Readers are fascinated by the contrast between a character's public facade and their true self, as well as the challenges they face in reconciling these identities while maintaining their love.
- Emotional Intensity: The Veiled Desires tropes elicit a heightened emotional response from readers. The hidden desires, secret yearnings,

and the risks involved in pursuing forbidden love evoke a sense of passion, longing, and sacrifice. The emotional intensity of these relationships resonates with readers, allowing them to experience a range of emotions vicariously through the characters.

POPULAR EXAMPLES OF THE VEILED DESIRES ROMANCE TROPES IN NOVELS IN 2022

In 2022, several novels embraced the Veiled Desires Romance tropes, captivating readers with stories of concealed identities and forbidden love.

One notable example is "The Masked Heart" by Emily Sullivan, where a noblewoman disguises herself as a servant to escape her stifling social constraints. In this tale of hidden desires, she falls in love with a mysterious stranger who is unaware of her true identity. The revelation of her secret and the challenges they face form the core of their tumultuous relationship.

Another compelling example is "Whispers of Deception" by Sarah Michaels, which follows a spy who infiltrates an enemy organization and finds herself torn between her loyalty to her mission and her growing feelings for a key member of the group. As secrets are unveiled and loyalties are tested, their love becomes entangled in a web of deception and danger.

ANALYZING THE VEILED DESIRES ROMANCE TROPES

The Veiled Desires Romance tropes offer readers a captivating exploration of secrecy, forbidden love, and hidden identities. By analyzing these tropes, we can identify recurring themes and elements that contribute to their appeal:

- Dualities and Contrasts: The Veiled Desires tropes often highlight the juxtaposition of different identities, contrasting social roles, or conflicting allegiances. This creates tension and intrigue, as characters must reconcile their true selves with the facades they present to the world. The exploration of dualities adds depth to the characters and their relationships.
- Consequences of Secrecy: The Veiled Desires tropes delve into the consequences of keeping secrets and the risks involved in pursuing forbidden love. Characters face moral dilemmas, emotional turmoil, and potential exposure as they navigate the treacherous path of concealed desires. The exploration of these consequences adds suspense and emotional depth to the narrative.
- Unveiling the Truth: The revelation of secrets and hidden identities is a pivotal moment in Veiled Desires romances. It marks a turning point in the relationship, leading to conflict, self-discovery, and the redefinition of love.

The process of unveiling the truth becomes a catalyst for character growth and the resolution of conflicts.

- Societal and Personal Barriers: Veiled Desires romances often confront societal barriers, such as class differences, political conflicts, or cultural norms. These barriers heighten the stakes of the relationship and challenge the characters' determination to overcome them. The triumph over societal and personal barriers reinforces the transformative power of love.

In conclusion, the Veiled Desires Romance tropes tap into the allure of secrecy, forbidden love, and hidden identities. Through popular examples in novels from 2022, readers are drawn into stories of concealed desires, dual identities, and the consequences of breaking societal norms. These tropes offer an intriguing blend of mystery, passion, and emotional depth, captivating readers as they eagerly unravel the secrets and witness the transformative power of love.

70
CONCLUSION
EMBRACING THE EXTRAORDINARY LOVE

The world of paranormal and supernatural romance is a captivating genre that allows readers to escape the confines of reality and embrace extraordinary love stories. Throughout this guide, we have explored various tropes and subgenres, each offering a unique blend of fantastical elements, intense emotions, and compelling character dynamics. From haunted destinies and forbidden love to time-defying relationships and veiled desires, these tropes have enchanted readers and inspired writers to create captivating narratives that transcend the boundaries of the ordinary.

In this final chapter, we will reflect on the allure of the paranormal and supernatural romance genre, explore the common threads that run through these tropes, and highlight the transformative power of embracing the extraordinary in love stories.

THE ALLURE OF PARANORMAL AND SUPERNATURAL ROMANCE

Paranormal and supernatural romance holds a strong appeal to readers for several reasons. Firstly, these stories allow us to break free from the constraints of reality and enter a world where magic, mythical creatures, and supernatural powers exist. This escapism offers a sense of wonder and adventure, transporting us to realms beyond our imagination.

Secondly, paranormal and supernatural romance explores the depths of human emotions in extraordinary circumstances. It delves into themes of love, sacrifice, redemption, and self-discovery, often pushing characters to their limits and testing the boundaries of their relationships. By immersing ourselves in these stories, we can vicariously experience intense emotions and witness the triumph of love over adversity.

Lastly, the genre provides a rich tapestry of diverse characters and relationships. From immortal beings and shape-shifters to witches and angels, paranormal and supernatural romance offers a plethora of unique and intriguing individuals. These characters navigate complex dynamics, cultural clashes, and personal transformations, allowing readers to explore different facets of identity, desire, and connection.

EMBRACING THE EXTRAORDINARY LOVE

At the heart of paranormal and supernatural romance is the concept of embracing the extraordinary in love. Whether it's overcoming personal demons, defying societal norms, or embarking on epic quests, the characters in these stories are faced with challenges that test the strength of their relationships and their capacity for growth.

Embracing the extraordinary love means accepting the unconventional, the magical, and the unknown. It involves delving into the depths of one's desires and fears, and finding the courage to pursue love in the face of obstacles and uncertainties. It is about breaking free from societal constraints and allowing oneself to be vulnerable and open to the extraordinary possibilities that love can offer.

By exploring these themes and tropes, writers can create narratives that resonate with readers on a profound level. They can craft characters who defy expectations, challenge the status quo, and ultimately discover the transformative power of love.

INSPIRING EXAMPLES AND WRITING TIPS

Throughout this guide, we have provided examples of popular books and movies within each trope, showcasing the creativity and ingenuity of writers in the paranormal and supernatural romance genre. These examples have demonstrated the diverse range of stories that can be told, from epic battles between supernatural beings to intimate and emotional journeys of self-discovery.

For writers looking to delve into this genre, here are a few tips to consider:

- Embrace Originality: While tropes provide a framework, don't be afraid to put your unique spin on them. Explore new angles, subvert expectations, and create fresh and compelling narratives that captivate readers.

- Develop Complex Characters: Strong character development is essential in paranormal and supernatural romance. Create characters with depth, flaws, and desires that resonate with readers. Allow them to grow, evolve, and confront their own inner demons as they navigate the extraordinary circumstances of their love story.
- Balance World-Building and Romance: Paranormal and supernatural romance often requires world-building to establish the rules and dynamics of the fantastical elements. However, ensure that the romance remains at the forefront of the story, driving the emotional journey of the characters.
- Tap into Emotion: Emotions are the heart and soul of romance. Infuse your writing with emotional intensity, exploring the complexities of love, desire, and sacrifice. Make readers feel the depth of the characters' emotions, creating a powerful and immersive reading experience.

THE TRANSFORMATIVE POWER OF EXTRAORDINARY LOVE

In conclusion, paranormal and supernatural romance offers a captivating blend of magic, mystery, and love. By embracing the extraordinary, these stories take readers on exhilarating journeys of self-discovery, redemption, and profound connection. Through the exploration of diverse tropes and subgenres, writers and readers alike are invited to step outside the boundaries of the mundane and immerse themselves in the transformative power of extraordinary love.

As writers, we have the privilege of weaving tales that transport readers to enchanted realms, allowing them to experience the magic and wonder that lies beyond the ordinary. By delving into the tropes and themes explored in this guide, we can create narratives that resonate deeply with readers, reminding them of the infinite possibilities and boundless beauty of love.

So, whether you're a writer seeking inspiration or a reader seeking an escape, embrace the extraordinary, and let the world of paranormal and supernatural romance transport you to realms where love knows no bounds.

ABOUT THE AUTHOR

E.B. Borbón is an emerging Paranormal & Supernatural Romance author with Speculative Historical References. Finding beauty in things forgotten and abandoned, he started to write short stories about the people, practices, beliefs, and places throughout history that fall between the well-known events. "The Fate of Eleonor" is E.B. Borbón's first published book.

facebook.com/e.b.borbon
instagram.com/e.b.borbon
goodreads.com/ebborbon

Made in the USA
Monee, IL
04 November 2026

67376085R00193